BUILDING CAREER EQUITY

How professionals and their firms achieve
mutual and meaningful growth

JAN TORRISI-MOKWA

© 2011 Jan Torrisi-Mowka. All rights reserved. This book may not be duplicated in any way without the express written consent of the author, except in the case of brief excerpts or quotations for the purpose of review. No part of this book may be reproduced or transmitted in any form or by any means (electronic, mechanical, photographic, recordings, or otherwise) without the express permission of the publisher, except for the inclusion of brief quotations in a review. The information contained herein is for the personal use of the reader and may not be incorporated in any commercial programs or other books, databases, or any kind of software without the written consent of the author. Making copies of this book or any portion of it for any purpose is a violation of the United States copyright laws.

ISBN: 978-0-9831896-7-1
Library of Congress Control Number: 2010919481

Book designed by Nehmen-Kodner: www.n-kcreative.com
Printed in the United States of America

Published by: Congruence Press
www.buildingcareerequity.com • email: jan@congruence-inc.com

To all those who make the choice, every day, to dream, learn, work, collaborate, give, and recognize others in pursuit of realizing their career aspirations.

Contents

Acknowledgments xi

Introduction 1

1 What Is Your Career Equity? 5

2 Doing Engaging Work 19

3 Cultivating Meaningful Relationships 33

4 Relentlessly Pursuing Learning and Growth 48

5 Contributing to Community 61

6 Reaping the Right Recognition and Rewards 74

7 Putting Action and Accountability Behind Aspirations 90

8 Cultivating a Career Equity Culture 101

Conclusions 127

Bibliography 133

Acknowledgements

The research, ideas, and writing that led to this book span more than eight years. During that time innumerable individuals and firms provided a context for learning, defining, and capturing the lessons you find in the pages that follow. I am grateful for their support, insights, and encouragement.

I am thankful to the partners and professionals of Arthur Andersen without whom this concept would not have been realized or developed. Specifically, I want to thank Larry Katzen who had the vision, courage, and dedication to embrace and invest in a new way of leading and developing professionals and for giving me the autonomy and authority to make it a reality. The firm's demise in 2002 provided an unintended context for testing how career-minded professionals adapt and adjust. While the loss of the culture and collaboration are dearly missed, nearly all of its members have found engaging work, meaningful relationships, and realized aspirations that in 2002 were not visible. They are a continuing inspiration and example of how building career equity comes to life.

I want to express my gratitude to the leaders of RubinBrown, Barry-Wehmiller's Design Group, Arcturis, Protiviti, Northwestern Mutual, and all the professionals like Tasha, Brett, Maggie, and Zundra who were willing to share their story so that others might learn and grow. They are career equity master builders and represent the essence of "meaningful relationships."

No book can be realized without the help and support of capable editors and publishing professionals. I am thankful for Noeli Lytton's editorial expertise, wisdom, and most importantly her affirming feedback when the voice of doubt crept in. Peggy Nehmen's creative design skills and mentoring on the publishing process were invaluable. Anyone publishing a book for the first time would benefit from her proactive sharing of articles, tips, and recommendations about the industry.

No significant goal is achieved without the support of interested colleagues and friends. I am thankful for Sabine Robinson's unwavering belief in the importance of this concept. Her experience as an author and consultant to the best financial service firms in the nation bolstered my belief in the value others would discover. She also generously shared ideas and tools which accelerated my work. I am appreciative of Wendy Werner's perspective as an advisor to the legal profession and her exceptional way of saying more with fewer words.

I am thankful to my mother Marie for her superior proofreading skills, objective perspective, and for teaching me the habits of expressing gratitude and professionalism throughout my life. Finally, to my husband Joe for his support, encouragement, and for keeping distractions of daily living at bay so I could have time to reflect and write. It is a gift to have a husband, mentor, and "appreciative audience" all in one person.

Introduction

The concept of Career Equity developed when I was at Arthur Andersen in 1997. The firm, like all professional service firms, experienced a high rate of turnover (nearly 24 percent) of the best and brightest associates. A strategic managing partner understood the correlation between high levels of effective client service and retention of top talent. Over the next three years, we worked with the firm's partners to erase double-digit turnover and build a culture of growth that benefitted each professional and the firm's business results. The process is repeatable and works.

Culture building began by interviewing professionals at every level of the firm—those new to the firm, equity partners, staff, and most importantly, those who left or were thinking of leaving. Each meeting helped me understand what compelled professionals to stay or go. Concurrently, we analyzed the firm's key-people processes (e.g., recruiting, orientation, training and development, and performance evaluations). We studied what professionals valued and which practices were unintentionally reinforcing an expectation of early career turnover.

Three key issues emerged from the research. First, less than 10 percent of professionals had a career vision. In other words, after completing the two-year experience requirement and achieving the credential of Certified Public Accountant (CPA), the majority of professionals had no clear plan for the long-term. We learned that when achievement-oriented professionals lack a career vision, it undermines their ability to make effective career choices in the present.

Secondly, we learned that when new career opportunities or dissatisfaction with a current career experience emerged, professionals did not naturally seek the counsel of a partner or owner who could affect a change in their situation. Rather, they sought guidance from peers or significant others. While seeking feedback from friends and family may seem logical and helpful, it is not optimal for making strategic career decisions. Family and friends do not have the power, influence, or authority to change career conditions. In other words, unless you are in a family-owned business, peers and family do not control your pay, progression, or assignments. Thus, the people who needed most to talk with each other (professionals and partners) were not doing so.

Finally, we learned that the firm's people-related business processes were not strategically integrated to help professionals see the relationship between their initial career goals, mentoring programs, training investments, and performance feedback or most importantly the link to firm business results. In other words, how my hard work contributes to firm success was vague. Significant time and resources were expended on these initiatives, prior to the Career Equity model, they were man-

INTRODUCTION

aged to achieve separate results. When a professional can't see the whole picture or how the firm seeks to help them advance, the firm's ability to leverage these investments diminishes.

Over several years of defining and implementing the Building Career Equity model we achieved a triple win. First, professional turnover dropped from 24 percent to less than 14 percent. This result occurred at the peak of the dot.com "War for Talent" not during an economic recession. Second, professionals had higher levels of satisfaction and a strategy they could discuss with partners and career advisors. Third, the career-oriented integrated framework improved our ability to attract new talent and better serve clients. We stopped the "revolving door" and provided greater continuity on client engagements. Professionals could see the value of their career experiences grow in tangible ways and clients didn't have new people on their account every six months.

Additionally, the firm's best people were watching. When they saw partners taking a sincere interest in the career growth of others, they were more proactive about sharing their career aspirations. Career decisions that were once isolated became more collaborative. A virtuous cycle of growth was created and sustained.

Today, the issues professionals face in defining and achieving their long-term career goals remain the same, and caring firm leaders are still in pursuit of win-win solutions. The firms that are "best practices" in Chapter 8 utilized the lessons learned at

Andersen and successfully applied them to their own culture. The results have been equally significant.

If you are a professional seeking greater career growth, I hope this book serves as a catalyst for you to think, discern, and most importantly take action on proven strategies that have helped other professionals achieve more of their career goals. If you are a firm leader, harness the lessons learned and make professional career growth part of your business strategy.

Either way, enjoy and if you find value, commit to teaching these practices to others. As Stephen R. Covey has helped me realize, teaching others leads to the highest level of self-awareness and effectiveness.

1: What Is Your Career Equity?

"If one advances confidently in the direction of his dreams, and endeavors to live the life which he has imagined, he will meet with a success unexpected in common hours."
—Henry David Thoreau

If you are reading this book, it is likely that someone who cares about you recommended it, or you found it researching strategies to enhance career growth. In either case, you are a Career Equity Builder.

What Is Your Career Equity?

Career Equity is a way of thinking, a framework, or paradigm about your career. It resonates most with those who possess or aspire to a calling requiring special knowledge and intense academic preparation. In short, anyone who considers him or herself a professional and is deliberate about building a meaningful career is accumulating Career Equity.

Building Career Equity offers a set of proven steps to increase clarity, career satisfaction, and tools that when implemented consistently accelerate the value of your career. It inspires professionals to evaluate how career investments are adding up and where opportunities exist to increase career effectiveness.

We know professionals spend as much as 60 percent of their waking life at work, yet fewer than 20 percent use systematic and strategic tools to manage their career. When was the last time you sat down and reviewed all of your career accomplishments and career aspirations with a career advisor? In financial matters, a disciplined process of planning, researching, working with a trusted advisor, and of course implementing the plan, leads to greater results. Those who implement Career Equity discover the same rewards in their career. Why is it that more than 80 percent of professionals don't have long-term written career plans nor do they regularly review it with an advisor? I believe the root of the issue is a lack of a holistic and systematic way of thinking about one's career that is shared and understood by our career advisors.

Most of us manage our careers incrementally. We evaluate career choices based on the opportunity in front of us. Shall I stay or go from this firm? Do I like or dislike working with the partner in this practice? Career Equity helps us take a longer view. Career Equity builders envision their future career and then design, document, and implement a comprehensive plan to achieve them. They know that absent a framework for guiding career decisions, short-term external factors such as discontent with a project, conflict with a manager or peers, or a competing salary offer can derail their long-term aspirations. While no plan is perfect and unplanned external factors (e.g., job loss due to

WHAT IS YOUR CAREER EQUITY?

economic downturns) do happen. Career Equity builders take initiative for career choices and thus avoid impulsive career changes and the regret of irregular career growth.

This book offers the strategies to achieve more of the career growth and satisfaction you desire by managing five key elements or assets. These assets when defined, reviewed, and implemented consistently lead to exceptional results. Your Career Equity is comprised of five assets: 1) Doing Engaging Work, 2) Cultivating Meaningful Relationships, 3) Relentlessly Pursuing Learning and Growth, 4) Contributing to Community, and 5) Reaping the Right Recognition and Rewards.

What follows are real-life stories, tools, strategies, and action plans for building your Career Equity. Part of being an effective Career Equity Builder begins with awareness of the daily choices you make to build and replenish one of the most important assets in your life. To get career growth underway, let's begin with a few questions:

1) **Who do you know that does a great job of managing their career?** In other words, they are clear about where they want to go and work strategically to get there. Write down the top two or three people who embody these traits.
   1. Nino Clarkin/Patrick Clarkin
   2. Steff Dutton
   3. Lori Smith

2) **Now consider what characteristics these professionals demonstrate that you admire?** What do they do that makes them come to mind and why are they so effective?

Were any of the following on your list?
- Invest time on their career goals and plans
- Define a compelling vision about where they want to be in the future
- Seek out mentoring and feedback to learn and grow
- Relentlessly invest in learning and developing new skills or knowledge
- Give generously of their time and talent to build a better community for all

Career Equity builders are strategic, thoughtful, engaged, and purposeful in managing most things in their life, especially their career. If you choose to fully implement the ideas and recommendations that follow, you will develop these characteristics and more. Again, by reading and investing the time to think and act on your career aspirations in a new way means you are well on your way.

A Career Equity Builder Example

At 7:30 A.M. on a Saturday, I was meeting with Tasha to discuss her next career opportunity. The meeting was happening because Tasha took the initiative to set it up. Tasha and I met

WHAT IS YOUR CAREER EQUITY?

initially when she was pursuing her undergraduate degree in human resources (HR) and I was the director of Human Resources at Arthur Andersen. She wanted to gain practical experience in HR through an internship and had come to me through a referral from a member of the local chapter of the Society of Human Resource management (SHRM). I share these details because they are evidence of behaviors that determine who achieves career goals and those who do not. Thinking about future career goals, taking initiative to meet with a "trusted advisor," involvement in a professional organization, and pursuing skill development through an internship are all evidence of Career Equity building skills.

This morning, more than seven years after our initial connection, Tasha wanted to discuss an offer she received to work at The Boeing Company. Tasha was utilizing me as one of her **Career Board of Directors** (discussed in Chapter 2) to help her assess how this opportunity aligned with her longer-term goals and the best strategy for negotiating a salary and benefits that would be a win-win for her and the company.

We discussed how a career at The Boeing Company would help Tasha accumulate more Career Equity. She determined this opportunity would give her experience in one of the world's largest and most reputable companies, access to world-class learning experiences, and the challenge of developing and implementing people solutions in dynamic organization and industry. Tasha had specific questions about how the culture of

Boeing might differ from her prior career experiences in smaller organizations and what she could do to manage the transition to such a large company more effectively.

A few days after our meeting, I received a heartfelt handwritten note from Tasha which expressed her gratitude for my time: another attribute of Career Equity builders.

I also received a follow-up email from Tasha, outlining the key points she took away from our meeting and a plan for acting on the things we discussed. I love this. Without prompting or management from me, Tasha was in charge of her career.

A few weeks later, I received another update from Tasha letting me know that she had accepted the position and was excited about beginning this new dimension of her career.

Whether you are looking for a new career opportunity or interested in expanding Career Equity in your current role and organization, Tasha's story is a great road map. Like Tasha, a good place to begin is by taking stock of the equity you have already acquired and where you have the opportunity to increase your career growth.

To gain a better understanding of your Career Equity, take a few moments and answer the following questions about your current career situation. The assessment can also point to the chapters in the book most relevant to you now.

WHAT IS YOUR CAREER EQUITY?

The Building Career Equity Assessment

The Building Career Equity assessment helps professionals identify where important career assets are accumulating and where opportunities exist to achieve a higher return. Since effective career growth never occurs in a vacuum, the completed assessment provides a practical tool for discussing career growth with interested managers, mentors, and advisors.

Using a scale where 5 = very true for my career today, 3 = somewhat true for my career today, and 1 = not at all true for my career today, read each of the statements and place the appropriate rating in the bcx to the right of the statement. Then total the number of points at the end of each asset category. Follow the directions below to see what your Career Equity Assessment is telling you.

Career Equity Assessment In Action

Career Equity is achieved by purposeful action, persistence, and patience. The following is a guideline for evaluating your Career Equity and asset accumulation in each category:

- Scores between 45 and 50, in a category, indicate an exceptional level of career investment and development. You are purposeful and thoughtful about growing your career results. You should be mentoring others in how to achieve more of their career goals.

BUILDING CAREER EQUITY

Career Asset #1 Doing Engaging Work	Scale of 1–5
1. My work challenges me intellectually, socially, and emotionally	3
2. I take initiative to seek out information about new projects and strategies my company or firm is pursuing	4
3. The work I do provides opportunities to gain new skills, knowledge, or experiences	2
4. I have a high level of variety in my work	2
5. I feel energized and enthusiastic about the work I do	3
6. I have a clear written vision for my career	3
7. I have a high degree of autonomy in my work	5
8. I have the right resources (materials, equipment, etc.)	4
9. People I work with are concerned about the challenge my work offers	2
10. I know where my talents best fit the needs of the organization	3
Total Points for This Asset (50 possible)	31

WHAT IS YOUR CAREER EQUITY?

Career Asset #2 Cultivating Meaningful Relationships	Scale of 1–5
1. I care about the people I work with	2
2. I have a network of professionals who are willing to help me grow and learn	3
3. My opinion matters to others I work with	3
4. There is at least one person in my life who encourages my career growth	4
5. I have a best friend at work	3
6. In the past six months, I have taken the initiative to discuss my career goals with a leader in my company or firm	2
7. I have developed at least one mentoring relationship where I work	1
8. I have developed at least one mentor outside my firm or company	3
9. I solicit open, honest feedback about my performance on a regular basis	3
10. I express gratitude in a tangible and meaningful way to those who invest in my growth	3
Total Points for This Asset (50 possible)	27

BUILDING CAREER EQUITY

Career Asset #3 Learning and Professional Growth	Scale of 1–5
1. I read at least one book or magazine a month to advance my professional skills and knowledge	3
2. Annually, I create a professional growth and development plan with specific measurable goals for learning (e.g., 20 hours)	2
3. I can articulate my strengths and the things that energize me at work	3
4. I know what differentiates me from other professionals in my area of expertise and am working to build this brand	4
5. In the past six months, I have taken the initiative to talk with someone about my professional development or learning goals	3
6. I serve as a teacher or facilitator in training others at least once a year	4
7. I complete a self-evaluation of my performance annually	3
8. I know my areas for development and a written plan of action to develop them	2
9. My leaders help me identify work assignments or projects that address my areas of development	1
10. My training and development plan is linked to the strategic needs of the organization I work for or aspire to work for	1
Total Points for This Asset (50 possible)	26

WHAT IS YOUR CAREER EQUITY?

Career Asset #4 Contributing to Community	Scale of 1–5
1. The organization I work for is respected in the community	4
2. I can articulate the two or three ways I would like to make a difference in the world or my community	3
3. I have written goals for community involvement this year	2
4. I am on the Board or committee of a not-for-profit organization	5
5. I invite others to participate in community activities or events	3
6. I have been recognized by a community organization for my efforts	2
7. I believe community involvement enhances career growth and progression	4
8. I solicit feedback from mentors/advisors on opportunities for community involvement	1
9. The place I work has a clear Purpose / Mission and Values that align with my values	3
10. I attend an "off-hours" community event at least once a month	1
Total Points for This Asset (50 possible)	28

BUILDING CAREER EQUITY

Career Asset #5 The Right Rewards and Recognition	Scale of 1–5
In the past month, I received recognition or praise for my work	5
I know the market value of pay and benefits for my position and experience	2
I use at least 70 percent or more of my vacation time annually	5
I participate in a 401K program or other retirement-savings plan	5
I am fully informed about my health care benefits; medical, dental, life insurance, long-term disability	2
I am satisfied with my level of compensation – base pay	3
I have a high degree of flexibility in choosing when I take time off for vacation, etc.	5
My organization makes contributions to charities or organizations I believe in	1
The people I work with want me to succeed and advance	2
In the past month, I have given recognition or praise to a co-worker	3
Total Points for This Asset (50 possible)	33

WHAT IS YOUR CAREER EQUITY?

- Scores that fall between 35 and 44, in a category, indicate progressive career growth. You are advancing and building assets, but a little extra intention would take your investments to the next level.
- Scores that fall between 25 and 34, in a category, indicate moderate Career Equity building. You would benefit from a higher level of focus and attention. Take the initiative to review your assessment with a career mentor or advisor in the next 30 days and formulate an action plan to work in one area immediately.
- Any category total of 24 or less indicates low-asset return, a need for greater intention, planning, and accountability. Pick one asset area that demands attention and create a plan to increase the results in the next year. Review your plan monthly.

While having exceptional scores in every area seems desirable, it is not typical. Those who are purposeful about Building Career Equity over the long-term identify the vital few areas where they want to accumulate significant assets and work to do so!
- What stands out to you about the current state of your Career Equity? *All areas are fairly moderate.*
- Which of the assets yielded the highest number of points? *Awards*
- Which asset needs immediate attention? *Professional Growth*
- Which statement caught your attention? *Friends at Work*

Armed with greater awareness about where you are now, you can focus on where you want to be in the future and how to do work that engages you.

Extra Credit

At the end of each chapter you will discover tools, ideas, and resources to accelerate the learning and application of the Career Equity building process. Here are a few to get you started:

1) Share the Career Equity assessment with a friend or colleague, have them complete the assessment, and compare results.
2) Share your Career Equity assessment results and action plan with a coach or mentor and get their feedback on next steps.
3) Read Lawrence G. Boldt, *How to Find the Work You Love* (New York: Penguin Group, 1996) or Timothy Butler and James Waldroop, *Discovering Your Career in Business* (New York: Perseus Books, 1996).

2: Doing Engaging Work

"Being busy does not mean real work. The object of all work is accomplishment and to this end there must be forethought, system, planning, intelligence, and honest purpose, as well as perspiration. Seeming to do is not doing."

—Thomas A. Edison

What Work Most Energizes And Engages You?

Mihály Csíkszentmihályi, in his seminal work, *Flow: The Psychology of Optimal Experience*, reveals that people experience super satisfaction when they are in a state of flow. Flow is a state of concentration or complete absorption with an activity in which the person is fully immersed and has a feeling of energized focus and full engagement. Time flies. Every action, movement, and thought follows inevitably from the previous one. In "flow" the emotions are not just channeled, but positive, energized, and aligned with the task at hand.

Does your work produce "flow"? What percent of the time do your professional experiences bring satisfaction, energy, and enthusiasm? Building Career Equity is about increasing the percentage of time you realize career satisfaction or "flow." While no work brings one 100 percent satisfaction, those who are purposeful about aligning what they do best to a particular need in the world are the most satisfied.

The asset of doing "engaging work" represents about forty percent of overall career satisfaction and effectiveness. In other words, if the nature of your work is not fulfilling, it is likely your Career Equity feels diminished.

How did you score on the Finding and Doing Engaging Work Assessment in Chapter 1? Research indicates that those who achieve 35 points or more (or approximately 70 percent favorable responses) realize three interrelated career benefits.

First, they report being happy or satisfied at work. Second, because they are more satisfied, they attract more and different opportunities. This is the "self-fulfilling" component of engaging work. The more you do great work the more you gain. Third, those who do engaging work are more likely to stay in their role or with their firm. This retention results in greater continuous experience. Instead of moving from job to job every six months, those who cultivate engaging work realize the reward of seeing their work through to completion.

Paradoxically, career persistence produces greater opportunities for career advancement. In other words, current and future employers recognize and desire people who stay engaged and achieve results. So doing engaging work translates into a higher probability of new career opportunities and career advancement.

If you feel you work hard but lack joy or fulfillment from your work, ask yourself three questions: Do I have a clear vision or definition of what engaging work means? Is there a high degree of fit or congruence between my unique skills and capabilities and the work I do? Finally, do I have an appreciative audience or people who value the contributions I make? The next section offers solutions and tools to help you find answers.

Creating a Clear Career Vision of Engaging Work

"There is more to us than we know. If we can be made to see it, perhaps for the rest of our lives, we will be unwilling to settle for less."

—Kurt Hahn

The most important aspect of achieving great results, in any context, begins with clarity of what we want to achieve. This is especially relevant for building Career Equity. Much has been written about the importance of a vision or definition of an ideal future. Yet, despite the number of articles and books research reveals fewer than 20 percent of professionals have clearly articulated what matters most to them. What is your ideal career? What do you want to be doing five years from now?

Without a vision or long-term goals, we run the risk of expending time, energy, and talent without realizing a feeling of success. Have you ever tried to do a puzzle without a picture on the box? While some find it mentally challenging, most people become frustrated and quit. Creating a vision is a picture of a personal ideal. It guides our choices and increases belief in our ability to achieve what matters most. We know from research in personal and organizational development that thinking and writing a vision increases the probability of achieving it.

A perfect example of a Career Equity builder and one who knows the power of a vision is Joe Cirulli. Joe's story "The Believer" appeared in the (August 2008) issue of *Inc.* magazine.

Joe is the CEO of three fitness clubs and four rehabilitation centers in Gainesville, Florida. His vision is to "keep Gainesville the healthiest city in America—one person, one business, one child at a time." He and his organization are well on their way to achieving this. Joe's inspiration came from reading one of my all-time favorite books, *Think and Grow Rich* by Napoleon Hill. From this book, Joe learned that the secret to success is in knowing what you want.

Joe took the time to write down ten goals for his life. Most importantly, as Napoleon Hill recommends, Joe reviewed the list every morning and every night for the next few years. Notice, I did not say days, weeks, or months but years! It is the mental rehearsal of aspirations that seem too big and too far that turns them into reality.

Joe's vision included ten key aspirations:
1) Own a health club in Gainesville
2) Make it respected in the community
3) Earn $100k by the age of twenty-five
4) Own a Mercedes-Benz, like the one driven by the Six Million Dollar Man
5) Own a home in the mountains, another one near the ocean, and build a home for his parents
6) Become a black belt

DOING ENGAGING WORK

7) Become a pilot and own a plane
8) Travel all over the United States
9) Travel all over the world
10) Save $1 million

It did take Joe over ten years, but he has accomplished every one of the goals on his list and more.

What is your career vision? Joe envisioned what career success meant to him in very specific terms and then acted in a systematic way to achieve them. Joe's path was not free from challenges or barriers. But in the process of pursuing his goals, Joe mastered an additional skill that enables Career Equity builders to create more of the engaging work they desire. That skill is the ability to suspend disbelief. To fully realize your career potential and find the work most engaging, you must quiet the little voice inside that whispers or at times shouts "you can't do that."

Suspending Disbelief

One of my favorite quotes about the correlation between belief and achievement is by the founder of Ford Motor Company. Henry Ford built one of the largest companies in the world from nothing. He was quoted as saying "whether you think you can or you can't, you are usually right."

The value of a vision is best observed in reverse or by looking backward. When we are setting out or beginning a new career, the prospect of achieving it may seem dim. It is our ability to suspend this disbelief that enables us to act and move forward. One of my best clients calls this act—faith. The difference between those who do engaging work and those don't is determined by their belief in the ability to see the unknown.

One tool for developing your vision and counteracting disbelief is called the three-year letter. The value of this tool came home to one in a poignant way when a client and friend died unexpectedly. Jim was a true professional, among the top 5 percent of all financial representatives.

Jim believed in the power of setting long-term goals for his career and life. Jim achieved significant results because he had a clear picture of career success and the ability to suspend disbelief. Jim was also a quiet leader. He was not one to shout his goals out publicly, but rather he reflected on what he wanted and acted with purpose to achieve it. After his funeral his son, who is one of the top management leaders in Northwestern Mutual, and I were discussing Jim's approach to life. Matt mentioned that going through Jim's papers, the family found a "three year career letter" Jim had written several years before. Matt was delighted that many of the aspirations his father defined were achieved. While we never know the time we are given, we can use our time and talent in the highest and best way, like Jim, by defining and acting on our vision.

.

Career Equity Tool: Three-Year Career Letter
While you can define a Career Vision for the next five or ten years, most professionals find three years a good place to begin.

DOING ENGAGING WORK

The key is to define the type of work that is engaging to you as specifically and clearly as you can. The more specific you are, the more likely you are to achieve it. Write your vision or letter in the present tense—seeing, feeling, and believing that the aspirations are achieved. In other words, write the letter assuming you have achieved success.

After you write your letter make a promise to review it every few months and share it with a mentor or career advisor.

Here is a template to get you started:

> *Dear (insert your name or someone important to you),*
>
> *It is now (fill in date three years from today), I have achieved a number of the aspirations I defined in (fill in today's date). When I wrote this letter three years ago, I wondered if these goals were really possible. Today, I can see how my commitment, hard work, and courage to define my goals in specific ways contributed to my success.*
>
> *The work I am doing is engaging and interesting. Specifically, I enjoy…*
>
> *The people who have most helped me achieve these career goals are…*
>
> *Continuous learning and growth were essential to advancing my career. The lessons I have learned are…*

> *The most beneficial and rewarding lesson was...*
>
> *Giving back to others was a key element of my plan. I believe in the principle—give first and generously. For example, ...*
>
> *I am reaping great rewards for my hard work and dedication to my goals and helping others succeed. My income is now...*
>
> *The recognition that matters most to me is... Other less tangible rewards include...*

Fit or Congruence Between Skills, Passion, and Work

"Where the needs of the world and your unique talents intersect is where you find your calling."

—Aristotle

In the international best seller *Good to Great,* author Jim Collins identifies that the most successful organizations or "great companies" do something good companies do not. They focus their time, talent, and resources on one thing they can do "best in the world." They do not try to be everything to everyone.

The same principles apply to doing engaging work. Knowing what you are or can be the best at in the world is the foundation of engaging work. What are, as Aristotle says, your unique

DOING ENGAGING WORK

talents? Do you possess the skill or ability for photography, architectural design, or accounting? What are you passionate about doing? What have others told you about your gifts or natural abilities?

A great tool for identifying unique skills and passions is to list of all the work you have done in the past (see table on page 28). Start with your first job. Did you babysit, cut lawns, or wait tables? Wherever your career journey began, make a list of all the things you enjoyed about this work in one column and then all of the things you disliked about the work or role in a second column. Repeat this for every job.

As you outline your career experiences you will begin to see patterns and themes. For example, you may see a theme about working with people in a helping or service capacity. Or perhaps solving problems or selling concepts are common elements in the work you have found most engaging. Ask yourself, how can I do more of the work that you enjoy? If you see a pattern or theme that does not appear in your current role or work don't be alarmed and certainly don't abandon your work —yet. In my experience "The grass is often greenest where it is watered." In other words, there may be a number of career opportunities awaiting you in your current organization or role that need to be more fully developed.

Maggie is a CPA with a passion for building personal relationships and addressing the unique needs of individual clients on tax-related matters. She discovered that a "Family Office" was a

Career Congruence Tool

	Type of work	What I enjoyed about this work:	What I disliked about this work:
First Job			
Second Job			
Third Job			
Etc.			

great fit for her talents and aspiration to grow a business within her firm. Her strong interpersonal skills, knowledge of tax law, and organizational abilities were a perfect fit for the firm's high wealth clients. Maggie took the initiative to approach her partners with the idea of establishing a "Family Office" practice.

She conducted research about the unique needs of wealthy families and the intergenerational wealth-transfer issues these families face. She asked to be the lead on several client matters to build her practical experience and test her assumptions about this specialized work. Three years after finding and doing this engaging work, Maggie remains energized about the support and counsel she provides clients who are making big decisions about the financial future of their children, grandchildren, and generations to come. The reward for discovering and pursuing this passion: Maggie is on track for even greater leadership roles—including partnership.

An Appreciative Audience

Another component of doing engaging work involves surrounding ourselves with people who can help us more fully realize our unique talents. In her book *Necessary Dreams,* author and psychiatrist, Dr. Anna Fels, says "the wish for mastery is undoubtedly a key component of ambition and success. But the pursuit of mastery virtually always requires a specific context: an evaluating, encouraging audience must be present for skills and talents to develop."

Who is your appreciative audience? Who encourages you to try new things, affirms your ideas or dreams?

Recently, as part of work with an international accounting firm, I interviewed each member of a large engagement team. Our discussions focused on how the firm helped them achieve their career aspirations and what kept them energized and committed to the firm's goals. The responses of one staff person stood out in my mind. When I asked her what motivated her to stay with the firm, she pulled out a notecard from her portfolio. On it was a handwritten message from a partner who was her mentor. She told me that last year, she was working on a big project for a very demanding client and deadlines were tight. "The partner took the time during this intense project to tell me how much he appreciated my commitment and dedication. It made me feel so important to the team and the firm." This staff person's work and dedication were noticed by leaders and increased her feeling of career engagement.

Note to firm leaders:
A handwritten note to members of your team during challenging projects is an antedote for turnover and supports team members long-term aspirations.

In my experience, the presence or lack of an appreciative audience correlates directly with the extent to which we describe our work as engaging. This element also links tightly with the next chapter on cultivating meaningful relationships. The key point here is that our satisfaction or engagement is influenced by the people we work with. If we believe our co-workers and leaders care about us and appreciate our contributions, we will find work more engaging. Conversely, the lack of an appreciative audience often predicts dissatisfaction and ultimately departure.

Having an appreciative audience doesn't always mean getting positive feedback. Some of the best growth and learning comes from leaders who are willing to provide challenging feedback.

Telling the truth is a far greater gift, even when it is not easy; as this senior associate learned in his mid-year review:

"I have a lot to improve on to achieve a promotion to manager. I wouldn't have known this if Ray did not take the time and have the courage to tell me what I didn't want to hear in my performance review. In reflecting on what he said, I had to agree with most of it. I wouldn't have gotten this out of it if he was sugarcoating."

Those who possess a high degree of engaging work and Career Equity know they can not wait passively for others to praise their work. Recognition is earned and reciprocal. If you want more you must give more. Giving a high degree of energy, enthusiasm, and engagement on a project precedes appreciation. Finally, when was the last time you were an appreciative audience for your co-worker or even boss? Reciprocating with genuine recognition to others not only strengthens work relationships, it increases our energy and satisfaction.

Doing Engaging Work is achieved by having a clear and compelling direction for your career future or vision. Ideally, your vision is written and reviewed frequently to help suspend the natural disbelief that occurs during the pursuit of bold goals. Additionally, your clarity about your unique skills and capabilities increases the probability of doing work that utilizes those strengths. Finally, engaging work depends on the people with whom we work. Co-workers, clients, or leaders providing feedback enhances career growth, affirming our aspirations. With a clear vision, congruence between skills and work, and an appreciative audience, we accumulate the value of interesting work with less effort and more "flow."

Extra Credit

1) Read Bo Birlingham, "The Believer," Inc. (August 1, 2008)
2) Read Napoleon Hill's *Think and Grow Rich*—especially Chapter 2, New York: The Random House Publishing Group, 1960.
3) Complete Career Assessment on page 28 and share with a mentor or career advisor.

3: Cultivating Meaningful Relationships

"There is no such thing as a self-made person. You reach your goals only with the help of others."

—George Shinn

"I was ready for a new challenge and reached out to a woman business owner I admired for career guidance. During the breakfast meeting at her club, she pointed across the room to a business leader she knew was looking for a senior executive to help him grow his firm. She got up, brought him over to meet me, and made a generous introduction about my skills and experience. Later that same day, he called me to schedule a time to meet and discuss the opportunity he was trying to fill. Three months later, I was fully employed in one of the most satisfying roles in my career. Without this connection and relationship, one of the best parts of my career would have never happened."

This professional's story is full of evidence about why meaningful relationships are one of the best predictors of career opportunity, satisfaction, and advancement. It points to the importance of taking the initiative to seek feedback from leaders we admire and being open to new career directions.

BUILDING CAREER EQUITY

Who shares ideas or resources that enable you to look at an issue from another perspective? Who cares enough to provide a great testimonial about your career accomplishments or offer challenging feedback the things you don't want to hear but need to hear?

Marcus Buckingham, author of the acclaimed *Now, Discover Your Strengths*, surveyed more than 20,000 professionals in diverse industries. His research reveals that the primary predictor of career satisfaction and effectiveness isn't technology, training, or the company you work for. It is the quality of a relationship with a manager or leader.

The absence of meaningful relationships at work is costly. Exit interviews with more than 1,000 employees at a large international accounting firm revealed that a lack of a meaningful relationships leads to turnover more than 80 percent of the time.

Finally, Mark Granovetter's classic study in *Getting a Job* underscores the importance of relationships in pursuit of new career opportunities. Granovetter researched employment histories of hundreds of professionals and technical workers in Boston. He discovered that 60 percent of those who found a new job did so through a personal connection not through an Internet search.

For all of these reasons and more, cultivating meaningful relationships is essential to Building Career Equity.

Current Career Advisors

Name	Expertise	Organization and Role	Age	Gender	Race	Met last
Example: Rachel Smith	Health Law	Partner at Smith and Burns	32	F	W	Dec. '08

Taking Stock Of Meaningful Relationships

Do you have the relationships you need to learn and grow in new directions?

Now is a good time to take stock of relationships that matter most to your professional life. Developing diverse and relevant relationships demands attention and intention. Professionals who have deep Career Equity make relationship building a priority and take the initiative to keep them current.

Social network theory tells us that the shape of a network determine its usefulness. Small, tighter networks are less useful than networks with multiple connections. More open networks introduce more new ideas and opportunities than closed networks with many redundant ties. In other words, a group of friends who only do things with each other share the same knowledge and opportunities. A group of individuals with connections to other social worlds have access to a wider range of information.

Clearly, we enjoy affiliating with people who have common values and interests. However, when professional networks are limited to "people like me," they limit career growth. Who are the current relationships in your Career Equity portfolio? Use the table on page 36 to capture the name and characteristics of relationships most meaningful to you now.

What patterns and themes do you observe about your current "meaningful" relationships? How diverse are their backgrounds? How do your aspirations align to theirs? When was the last time you let them know they make a meaningful contribution to your career?

Who Is "On Board" With Your Career?

Knowing where you stand today with current relationships is a critical first step in cultivating meaningful relationships. If your assessment reveals a high degree of diversity in organization, race, gender, age, and organizational level, you have a strong network that will serve you well. However, most professionals find these relationships are overrepresented in one industry, firm, age, race, and gender. This is an opportunity to expand relationship diversity. Just like an investment portfolio, diversity yields better results over the long-term.

When Kim was thinking of making a change in her career to corporate finance, she made a list of relationships in her network. Kim remembered that a regional leadership program she participated in gave her the opportunity to meet several finance professionals. Once Kim shared her plan with them, they were willing to introduce her to a chief financial officer (CFO) in a company she was targeting. Kim was surprised that connections developed outside of her immediate organization were the catalyst to realizing her career goals.

In *"Achieving Success through Social Capital"* author Wayne E. Baker reports that most Americans cultivate homogenous networks. Twenty percent of Americans talk with only one person about important matters. Some do not talk with anyone at all. In today's dynamic professional world, a small, homogeneous network does not provide adequate support nor optimize learning.

Cultivating meaningful relationships is not about quantity. It is about diversity and quality. It is about raising our awareness and intention of the great relationships we possess and the courage to build new ones. One tool for increasing the quality and depth of meaningful career relationships is to think of these people as a **Career Board of Directors.**

The Career Board of Directors: Advisors Who Help You Build Career Equity

"What every leader needs are advisors who will tell you the brutal truth even when it is something you don't want to hear."

—*Jimmy Carter, U.S. President*

Chief executive officers (CEOs) of public companies know the importance of diverse meaningful relationships. They often call these people the "Board of Directors." Boards are a necessity for a public company or a not-for-profit organization. They ensure that the public good or shareholder interests are met.

James Kristie, editor of the publication *Directors and Boards,* says, "The purpose of a Board is to offer their intelligence, integrity, and courage to exercise dutiful oversight of

CULTIVATING MEANINGFUL RELATIONSHIPS

management and contribute in meaningful ways to the strategic affairs of the enterprise." Without a thoughtful, engaged, and ethical conscience, the CEO can become distracted from her core purpose and put an organization, people, and personal careers in jeopardy.

Clearly, Boards steer the strategy and guide the success of an organization. How could this model benefit your career? Would a trusted group of individuals using their intelligence, integrity, and courage guide your career to better results?

How do you build a Career Board of Directors? For some professionals, a Career Board is very structured. They develop a formal process of inviting members to the Board, scheduling meetings, and reporting career goals and results. For others simply having this mental model adds substance to their career portfolio. The level of structure you choose for a Career Board is up to you.

However you proceed, thinking like the CEO of your career will expand your perspective and open you to different feedback. The following guiding principles have helped hundreds of professionals build or enhance their Career Board of Directors.

Quality, not size matters. Don't build a Board with 15 people. Look at your current relationship list and select one or two current advisors. Then add one or two new relationships that allow you to grow outside of your "comfort zone."

When recruiting people to your Career Board, ask yourself these questions: Will they be able to dedicate time to help me?

Highly visible business leaders are a great resource but they may be too busy.

Do they demonstrate the ability and courage to be open and honest? Deep relationships and learning come from open, honest feedback. A group of "yes" people will not produce the growth you are seeking. Identify people who will challenge you to look at the things you want to avoid.

Do they have diverse perspectives, backgrounds, or experiences? As we have discussed earlier, diversity is an important dimension of career success. Seek it.

Take a moment to list advisors you want to cultivate:

❏

❏

❏

❏

Many professionals get stuck at this point. They are comfortable identifying people who can add value but uncomfortable taking relationships to a deeper level. Asking people for guidance and time requires an emotional risk. Risk is a prerequisite to growth.

CULTIVATING MEANINGFUL RELATIONSHIPS

To move from thought to action, consider advice from Donna Fischer, author of *People Power: 12 Principles to Enrich Your Business, Career, and Personal Networks*. Fischer shares two best practices for building new relationships. First, she says be clear about what you want and how you think this person can help. For example, how often would you like to meet with them?

Clarity of purpose helps others help you. Your career advisors will be more effective if they are clear about what you are trying to achieve. Organize and prepare for your meetings in advance. Don't waste an advisor's valuable time with unstructured meetings and vague objectives.

A best practice to follow is the approach recently used by the CFO of a $300 million dollar company. He called me to give him feedback on how to increase his community involvement. He listed two or three criteria describing the type of organization he wanted to serve and the role he wanted to play. This type of pre-engagement creates a favorable impression and results in more specific actionable feedback.

Fischer's second suggestion is to tell potential advisors what is special about them and what caused you to ask for their help. This goes a long way toward cultivating meaningful relationships. Do you remember the last time someone asked you for help because of your special talents, knowledge, or gifts? How did you feel? People are flattered by your request. Even if they are too busy to serve as an advisor, they will respect you for asking.

A Career Equity Builder Example

"It was my fifth year as a financial advisor and I hit a wall. I was behind in my production goals, my assistant resigned, and my income was not sufficient to support my growing family. My first thought was to leave. Quit. Go back to a good job at Kodak as a sales manager. My managing partner knew I was struggling. He knew an outside perspective would increase the effectiveness of my decision making. He arranged a meeting with the firm's strategic business advisor. She gave me valuable feedback and strategies to help me persist during this difficult time. I also formed a "Board of Advisors" that was and continues to be an invaluable source of feedback and support. All of these relationships made a significant difference in my career decisions. I just celebrated my eleventh anniversary with the firm. I've achieved the industry's top sales award and will be opening my own district office this year. What is clear to me now is that without the mentoring and support from outside coaches and my advisory board, I would not have remained. I would have settled for something below my capabilities."

Fred's story perfectly illustrates the value of mentors and forming a Board of Advisors. Today, Fred is building his own district office and actively recruiting and mentoring others to achieve their career vision. Without feedback and support at a critical time, Fred may have made another decision and not realized his full potential in his profession.

Three Steps To Cultivating More Meaningful Relationships

After you recruit trusted career advisors, you will want to focus on retaining these meaningful relationships. The following three steps outline how to keep important relationships mutually beneficial.

Step 1: Listen. Stephen Covey's bestselling book *The Seven Habits of Highly Effective People* highlights the habit of "seeking first to understand, and then be understood." It is a critical habit in developing interdependence and strong relationships. Many professionals express that it is an attribute of tremendous value but difficult to master. When you have identified the relationships you want to cultivate. Make sure you listen.

Ask questions about their background, experiences, and lessons learned. Engage them by asking follow-up questions and taking note of their responses. You identified these individuals because of their skills, expertise, and unique perspective. Make sure you gain as much as you can by listening to and learning from their experiences.

Step 2: Ask and Act. Planning and analyzing are critical components of building Career Equity. However, *action* drives results. Many successful business executives believe that an idea 20 percent planned and 80 percent executed is superior to an idea 80 percent planned and 20 percent executed.

Ask for feedback and input from your trusted career advisors and then *act*. People will be more likely to contribute to your career growth if they see that you act on their guidance.

In addition, integrate your planning and acting by establishing a Career Advisor Connection Calendar. Plan ahead to meet with advisors and keep them informed of your accomplishments produces great results. Few business professionals want to be a career crisis counselor. Be proactive and stay in touch when things are going well, too.

Step 3: Acknowledge Contributions. When I was young, my mother taught me to send a thank you note within a few days of receiving a gift. A handwritten note of thanks, not an e-mail, is an expression people treasure. When someone gives you time and attention, it is a gift. Be sure you honor this with an expression of appreciation.

In summary, building a diverse Career Board of Directors will accelerate your career growth. Acting on their feedback and acknowledging their contributions will build more meaningful relationships and equip you with an essential component of Career Equity.

Career Growth By Helping Others Succeed

"It is one of the most beautiful compensations of this life that no one can sincerely try to help another without helping himself."

—*Ralph Waldo Emerson*

One of the most powerful ways to cement learning and continue growing meaningful relationships is to teach others what you have learned. Sharing your knowledge reflects a principle

CULTIVATING MEANINGFUL RELATIONSHIPS

of stewardship. Webster defines *stewardship* as: *"Conducting, supervising, or managing something; especially the careful and responsible management of something entrusted to one's care."*

Serving as a trusted career advisor for someone else is an act of stewardship that builds your skills and capacity to lead and develop others.

Mike, chief operating officer of a growing company, is responsible for growing and expanding four business units and knows the mutual value of helping others succeed. More than 20 years ago, Mike benefited from the patient coaching and guidance of a senior engineer named Jack. Mike says his meeting with Jack is as vivid as if it were yesterday.

"I was a new hire in engineering at Pfizer and was asked to replace a distillation column. I had no idea what a distillation column was. I went to Jack and admitted my shortcoming and braced myself for the standard "didn't they teach you that in college." Instead, Jack invited me into his office and spent more than 30 minutes creating detailed drawings and explaining the function of a distillation column and how to replace it. Jack didn't show off his knowledge. He truly cared about helping me."

Today, when one of Mike's protégés approaches him with what seems like a fundamental question, he remembers Jack's mentoring. He is careful not to dismiss their questions but takes the time to listen and teach them how to succeed.

Take a moment and reflect on protégés, colleagues, or family members who would benefit from developing their own Career Board. Who comes to mind?

If you mentor more than one person, you may want to consider bringing your protégés together in a Mentoring Circle. Mentoring Circles function like book clubs or discussion groups. Each month a member brings a topic for the group to read and discuss. Engage them in a dialogue of best practices on building relationships with career advisors.

At your next team meeting, you could discuss the concepts in this chapter and ask them to consider the relationships that are guiding their career. Is it time to schedule a Career Equity conversation with one of your best professionals? If your current role includes managing or developing others, you will want to read Chapter 8. There is nothing more motivating and effective than showing interest in a professional's career goals.

Extra Credit

1) Read Marcus Buckingham and Donald O. Clifton *Now Discover Your Strengths* (New York: The Free Press, 2001)

2) Read Donna Fischer *People Power: 12 Power Principles to Enrich your Business, Career, & Personal Networks* (Austin, TX: Bard Press, 1995).

3) Read Malcolm Gladwell *The Tipping Point: How Little Things Can Make A Big Difference* (New York: Little, Brown and Company, 2000).

4: Relentlessly Pursuing Learning and Growth

"A mind stretched to a new idea never goes back to its original dimensions."
—Oliver Wendell Holmes

"I have always been passionate about learning new things, but Australia was never part of my career plan. It turned out to be one of the best experiences of my life." This insight comes from Kathy, a certified public accountant (CPA) in a firm that offers international exchange opportunities to its best professionals.

Firm leaders invited Kathy to be part of an audit team in Sydney, Australia when she was beginning her third year on the audit staff. The assignment required a six-month commitment. She knew an experience in another country would give her unique learning and growth—differentiating her from other professionals. When Kathy returned from Australia, firm leaders were eager to hear what lessons she'd learned. The managing partner asked Kathy to share her experiences with all firm members at the Annual Meeting and create a YouTube video to share with potential recruits.

cat·a·lyst [kátt'list] n.
stimulus to change:
somebody or something that makes a change happen or brings about an event

Kathy's experience is a great example of the five learning catalysts Career Equity builders use to relentlessly learn and grow. In this chapter, we will describe each of the five learning catalysts and offer best practices to accelerate learning assets.

Catalyst 1: Be Open To New Opportunities

Kathy would not have realized exponential growth in technical, interpersonal, and leadership skills without being open to a new opportunity. While an international assignment sounds intriguing, it demands significant change in familiar schedules, work locations, relationships, and conveniences. Consider that Australia is on a different continent and fifteen hours ahead of the time when Kathy's family and friends are awake and working. Just calling a friend demands a new lexicon of international phone codes and mental gymnastics. Career Equity builders embrace new opportunities and seek situations that get them out of their "comfort zone." They exemplify Eleanor Roosevelt's wisdom: "Do one thing everyday that scares you."

However, you do not need to travel halfway around the world to embrace new learning and growth. In fact, new opportunities beckon us constantly. The key is to be aware of them and say yes to them when they are right for you. For example, when was last time your firm invited you to attend the local business journal breakfast seminar or video-conference on a new technical skill? Did you take advantage of the opportunity or persist with your familiar routine?

Opportunities abound if we are paying attention. A few years ago, I was in my friend Anne's office. Anne is a bank executive and her clients are business owners and CEOs. I noticed a brochure on her desk of a beautiful mountain ranch home. She told me "Last Chance Ranch" was in Aspen, Colorado and belonged to the CEO of a well-known company that had a strong relationship with the bank. She thought I would enjoy meeting him because he was very intent on building a values-driven organization and developing leaders.

Several weeks later, Anne created the opportunity for me to meet the CEO and the leader of his organizational change practice. Over the next year, the three of us met several times to discuss leadership and organizational-growth strategies. Eighteen months after seeing the brochure, I was invited to facilitate a discussion with six other CEOs on leadership development at the Aspen retreat I originally admired.

How are you attending to the things that energize and inspire you? How might a conversation open a door to a new learning or insight?

Catalyst 2: Participate In Professionals Associations
Are you a member of a nationally recognized professional association? If you are, how would you describe your level of

engagement or contribution? If you are like most professionals, you pay your annual dues and toss the complimentary magazine in the "read later" pile.

Professional memberships are often an underutilized Career Equity asset. Consider the following ways professional affiliations can build equity with a reasonable level of effort and intention:

1) Provide the latest technical or industry knowledge in magazines, web sites, journals, etc.
2) Increase the depth and breadth of your professional network, including access to senior leadership in your profession.
3) Offer a forum to increase your professional "brand" through speaking or writing opportunities.
4) Develop leadership skills by choosing to serve on a committee, task force, or in an officer role.

As we know from Chapter 1, Tasha discovered that involvement in a professional association opened new doors to career opportunities. She took the initiative to find the local chapter of the Society of Human Resource Management Association and didn't stop there. She researched the intern program and after several months of showing up and being a contributor, she contacted me at Arthur Andersen. Because Tasha invested time and energy in the Association she gained awareness of new opportunities and access to decision makers that she would not have without active involvement in this membership organization.

Catalyst 3: Mentoring

Mentoring has been around for centuries. In fact, we get the term *mentor* from Greek mythology. When Odysseus left for the Trojan War, he placed Mentor in charge of his palace and his son Telemachus to guide development of this emerging king. Gaining a mentor is a highly efficient and effective learning and growth strategy. One mentoring meeting yields numerous benefits. For example, a mentor can help you gain new technical knowledge, role play how to deliver challenging feedback to a team member, bolster your self-confidence, or think more strategically about long-term career opportunities.

In today's business world, mentors possess experience, expertise, or wisdom and a willingness to share this with another, typically less experienced, professional. **The Mentor Hall of Fame** (http://www.mentors.ca) compiled by Rey Carr includes examples of great business leaders and the mentoring advice they gained. The following are a few excerpts from Carr's list:

- Herb Kelleher (Founder and chairman of Southwest Airlines) was mentored by his mother Ruth, who told him, "Respect people for who they are, not for what their titles are."
- Benjamin Graham (Columbia University professor) and Howard Buffett (dad), mentors to Warren Buffett (CEO, Berkshire Hathaway), told him, "You're right not because others agree with you, but because your facts are right."

- Warren Bennis, mentor to Howard Schultz (CEO, Starbucks), suggested to his mentee, "Recognize the skills and traits you don't possess, and hire the people who have them."

Who are your mentors? What characteristics or attributes do they possess that are of value to you? What guidance have they given? As a Career Equity builder, it is unlikely you have arrived at this point without a mentor. As an asset, these meaningful relationships are essential. As a learning and growth strategy, they are a source of rich information and feedback peers may not have the courage or inclination to share.

How often are you soliciting mentor time and feedback? Do you prepare for this meeting to ensure that you are getting the most from their wisdom? What do you do after the meeting to ensure new learning or insights are acted on?

We often think of mentoring as benefitting the protégés. However, research reveals that the mentor gains as much if not more from a mentoring experience than the understudy. If you have several mentors, begin to think how you could learn and grow from mentoring others.

Catalyst 4: Cultivate Reading Rituals

"Those who cannot remember the past are condemned to repeat it."

—George Santayana, Spanish-American philosopher

RELENTLESSLY PURSUING LEARNING AND GROWTH

What motivates you to try new approaches in your work, community, life?

What resources do you read regularly to expand your knowledge and awareness of current or historical events? Here are mine. First, the *Harvard Business Review* and *Inc.* magazine have been reading rituals for more than a decade. These monthly periodicals are full of well-researched leadership and organizational strategies for growing companies. In every issue, I find at least one article that is relevant to my practice or my client's business.

Second, *The Wall Street Journal* is a learning source every business day. I read it before I leave for the first client meeting. Third, I end my day by reading *Leadership Promises for Every Day* by John C. Maxwell.

My friend and colleague Wendy Werner calls these resources "brain candy" or information that stimulates and excites our cerebral cortex. Reading keeps you professionally relevant and vital.

For example, after reading an article in *Leader to Leader*, a magazine published by the Drucker Leadership Institute, I learned that CEOs wanted to read and discuss leadership challenges. I approached eight to ten clients with this idea and the majority accepted immediately. I now host a quarterly CEO Book Club that expands my learning as well as others. The group's reading list includes diverse topics on leadership and organization effectiveness. The following is a small sample of the books and articles we've read:

BUILDING CAREER EQUITY

- Bo Birlingham, "The Believer," *Inc.* (August 1, 2008)
- Peter Drucker, *The Practice of Management* (New York: Harper Collins Publishers, Inc., October 1954) (written in 1945)
- P.M. Forni, *Choosing Civility: The Twenty-five Rules of Considerate Conduct* (New York: St. Martin's Press, February 2002)
- Stephen R. Covey, Bob Whitman, and Breck England, *Predictable Results in Unpredictable Times* (Salt Lake City, Utah, Franklin Covey, September 2009)

Finally, I set a goal to read one new book each month. This ensures I have a fresh supply of options for the Book Club as well as keeping my professional knowledge on the cutting edge. The magazines I read are my preferred sources for new book titles. If you are looking for a place to begin, The *100 Best Business Books of All Time: What They Say, Why They Matter, and How They Can Help You* by Jack Covert and Todd Sattersten is a great resource. Developing reading rituals will add depth and dimension to your continuous learning and growth.

Catalyst 5: Teach to Learn

Stephen R. Covey, the author of numerous best-selling books and the master of the *Seven Habits of Highly Effective People*, uses a strategy called "Teach to Learn." All FranklinCovey books and workshops utilize this method to enhance retention of knowledge.

The method is very easy to implement. Every time you learn something, summarize the key lessons learned and share the knowledge with someone else. Research indicates that successful learning, preparation, and teaching of others leads to greater self-esteem, social connections, and self-actualization. The repetition of information also increases retention by as much as 50 percent. As a Career Equity builder, teaching expands your knowledge and presents you as an expert in the subject matter. Every time you teach you develop a deeper appreciation for the content and others begin to recognize you as a resource for their own learning. Don't just be satisfied with learning it once, pass it on!

Zundra is a vice president at MasterCard Worldwide. Zundra and I met several years ago when I was a panelist on career advancement for the Professional Organization of Women (P.O.W.). Zundra is a master of Career Equity builder. She purposefully takes knowledge and information from one context and shares it. For example, Zundra is a leader of MasterCard's L.E.A.D. business resource group. L.E.A.D. is dedicated to helping MasterCard employees build knowledge and relationships to advance their careers. Because of the knowledge Zundra gained from our work together at P.O.W., she recommended me as a speaker for L.E.A.D. Now, MasterCard employees are utilizing Career Equity tools (e.g., the Three-Year Letter, Career Board of Directors, etc.). Because of Zundra's learning and growth, she provided other MasterCard professionals and managers with the new tools and resources to enhance their careers. Follow Zundra's example. Learn and pass it on!

Learning And Growth Tools

Now that you understand the five catalysts Career Equity builders use to continuously learn and grow, take a moment and capture how you have been implementing these factors in your career. List one or two examples which illustrate each Learning and Growth factor in the first column of the table on page 58.

After you complete the examples, identify the one area that would benefit from greater focus and attention in the next six months. Use the next tool, The Learning Log, to set your action plan in writing. Even a five percent increase in attention and intention will increase your Career Equity. Once you have established a set of learning goals for the year, create a way to track and record your learning investments. See example on page 58. It is also an effective record for professional organization's which require proof for accreditation and is a tangible mechanism for following-up on your intentions.

Extra Credit

1) Review Jack Covert and Todd Satterson, *The 100 Best Business Books of All Time: What They Say, Why They Matter, and How They Can Help You* (London: Bloomsbury Publishing Inc., 2003)

3) Read *The Seven Habits of Highly Effective People* by Stephen R. Covey.

4) Create a Learning Log and review it monthly.

RELENTLESSLY PURSUING LEARNING & GROWTH

Learning & Growth Factor	Example(s) in the past six months	Focus Area
Catalyst 1: Embrace new opportunities		
Catalyst 2: Seek and share best practices		
Catalyst 3: Mentor or be mentored		
Catalyst 4: Cultivate a habit of reading		
Catalyst 5: Teach to learn		

Learning Log Example

Event Descripiption	Date	Credits Hours	Status
Organizational Development Conference	May 13	4	*Completed*
Economic Update Forum	June 30	1.5	Completed
Survey Design Workshop	September 23	3.0	Register Online
Strategy Workshop – Washington University	November 20	8.0	Registered
Total Hours (goal of 40)		*16.5*	*50% of goal*

5: Contributing to Community

"A man of humanity is one who, in seeking to establish himself, finds a foothold for others who, desiring attainment for himself, helps others attain"

—Confucius

"My work is challenging, I like the people I work with, and I get numerous opportunities to learn and develop new skills, but the thing that really energizes me is the time I "give back" to the community. Last year, I participated in a Habitat for Humanity build. It was rewarding to know I was creating a home for a family who might not have one."

—Senior associate at a national architecture firm

Contributing to Community is the fourth element of building Career Equity. Today, successful professionals want more from their work life than accumulating career experiences and credentials. They want to know they are making a difference in the world. A recent survey of MBA students by The Aspen Institute and Net Impact, found 29 percent have an increased interest in a career in public service. The survey report cited three themes:

- Signs point to potential increased interest in government and nonprofit work among young people.

- Greater attunement to the roles of nonprofits and government may help MBAs to become better social and environmental stewards.
- Nonprofit management courses open students' eyes to the possibility for collaborative problem solving through cross-sector partnerships.

The interest in building Career Equity by contributing to the community is not isolated to MBA's. Nationally, 27 percent of 1.6 million graduating seniors plan to work for nonprofit groups or governments, an increase of 23 percent, according to a survey of 14,225 U.S. college students conducted by the National Association of Colleges and Employers, in Bethlehem, Pennsylvania.

Thirty-nine percent of graduates want private sector jobs, down from 45 percent in 2009. "There's a generational shift toward increasing interest and concern about how to help make the world a better place," Amherst College President Anthony Marx said. "I hear students saying, 'We want to make a difference and we're not going to feel quite right about ourselves if we don't do that.'" (Source: Bloomberg online, June 23, 2010). What do you believe about contributing to the community? Is it a fully realized or underdeveloped aspiration?

Giving Back Builds Skills

While public service and nonprofit positions fully integrate a sense of career meaning, it is not necessary to quit your job or change your career path to make a difference. Many professionals find community contribution outside their regular work day a source of fulfillment and skill building.

Research conducted by Markitects (2005) found statistical proof of a correlation between community service and career success. Eighty-three percent of respondents reported that leadership skills were honed through volunteer work and that this experience was directly transferable to their professional roles. Seventy percent of participants cited improved communication skills, and 66 percent mentioned they developed "hard skills" in fundraising and resource management. The findings indicate nonprofits and community-based endeavors are an important, informal training ground for business leaders today.

Let's revisit how you scored on this rewarding career asset. See your initial assessment results on page 15 or complete the assessment on page 62 to explore where opportunities exist to give back and build Career Equity.

When you review your assessment, what areas stand out as strengths? Where do you have opportunities to build Career Equity while helping others? The following section covers six key strategies for increasing effective community contribution.

Community Strategy #1: Know What Matters Most to You
Career Equity builders get involved and "give back." They know that doing something for the "greater good" brings

BUILDING CAREER EQUITY

Career Asset #4 Contributing to Community	Scale of 1–5
1. The organization I work for is respected in the community	
2. I can articulate the two or three ways I would like to make a difference in the world or my community	
3. I have written goals for community involvement this year	
4. I am on the Board or committee of a not-for-profit organization	
5. I invite others to participate in community activities or events	
6. I have been recognized by a community organization for my efforts	
7. I believe community involvement enhances career growth and progression	
8. I solicit feedback from mentors/advisors on opportunities for community involvement	
9. The place I work has a clear Purpose /Mission and Values which align with my values	
10. I attend an "off-hours" community event at least once a month	
Total Points for This Asset (50 possible)	

CONTRIBUTING TO COMMUNITY

multiple rewards. As mentioned previously, "givers" gain leadership skills while building new relationships and cultivating the intrinsic satisfaction of making a difference.

The issue for career-minded professionals is usually not whether to get involved but what and where to contribute. There are literally thousands of nonprofit organizations who are seeking volunteer time, talent, and treasure.

Which organization is an optimal fit for your skills, capabilities, and time? My guiding principle is to identify something you are passionate about. Consider how Brett and Julie found their passion and purpose founding *Swing Fore Hope*.

"*In 2003, when four close family members were diagnosed with breast cancer within a seven-month period, we were faced with the harsh reality that 50 percent of men and 30 percent of women will be diagnosed with cancer over the course of his or her lifetime.*

We decided to meet this issue head on by raising money for cancer research and treatment by starting Swing Fore Hope, *a 501 (C)3 nonprofit organization. Our main event is a golf tournament held at Sunset Hills Country Club in Edwardsville, Illinois. Each year, 100 percent of the proceeds go towards cancer research and education.*

Going on its fourth year, Swing Fore Hope *has collectively donated more than $100,000 to The American Cancer Society and The Siteman Cancer Center in St. Louis, Missouri. We are determined to make a difference.*"

Family experience with cancer motivated this young inspiring couple to give back. Like most Career Equity community contributors, Brett realizes additional benefits from this investment of time and talent. Brett is the managing director of the Gilliland Financial Group in Edwardsville, Illinois. *Swing Fore Hope* is a powerful team and client-building event. His entire organization is involved in planning, hosting, and having a good time on the links. Clients and community leaders participate. Every invitation and the *Swing Fore Hope* web site extend the mission and brand of his firm.

Rewarding community contribution begins with things that matters most to you. Personally, I have a passion for the humane treatment of animals. This enthusiasm and advocacy appeared early in my life. When I was thirteen, I organized a petition drive to support the efforts of the *Friends of Animals.* Their mission was to expose the tuna industry for using fishing nets that inadvertently caught and suffocated dolphins. Other nets were available that could save these brilliant mammals, but they were not being used. After several years of social and political pressure by the *Friends of Animals,* the industry changed its practices and millions of dolphins are now protected. As a teenager, this community contribution taught me the value of getting involved, taking initiative, and organizing for action can make a sustainable change. When was the first time you recall being passionate about creating change to make something better? What lessons did you learn? What skills or competencies did you develop that are relevant to your career and life now?

More recently, my passions for helping animals led me to the Humane Society of Missouri (HSMo). A few years ago, I was reading an article in *Inc.* magazine (more evidence of the value of continuous Learning and Growth) about a woman who sold designer purses on eBay and gave the proceeds to the local humane organization. I thought it was a great idea and sent the article to the HSMo executive director. She shared my enthusiasm for the idea and asked me to spearhead a committee to "raise friends" among professional women. *Purses for Pooches and Pals* celebrated its fifth anniversary in 2010. More than 400 women attend this fundraiser annually. Over the past five years, the team has raised more than $400,000 benefitting the Dr. Doolittle Fund, which provides veterinary care for homeless, abused, and neglected animals. This event would not be possible without a strong team. In addition to the joy of achieving a significant goal for animals, I have gained new relationships with amazing female leaders at Enterprise Rent-A-Car, AT&T, Brown Shoe Co., MasterCard International, and others.

Community Strategy #2: Research the Needs in the World

Wendy Kopp, founder of *Teach for America,* developed the idea to eliminate educational inequity in the United States when conducting research for her senior thesis at Princeton University in 1989.

BUILDING CAREER EQUITY

Since its beginning in 1990, more than 14,000 corps members have completed their commitment to Teach for America. The history of the organization is chronicled in her book *One Day, All Children: The Unlikely Triumph of Teach for America and What I Learned along the Way.*

Community contributors like Wendy Kopp remind me of Margaret Mead's saying, "A small group of thoughtful people could change the world. Indeed, it's the only thing that ever has." If you still struggle with where to "get involved" consider the following needs awaiting your talent:

- Over seven million homeless pets in the United States need a good home.
- Most disaster fatalities happen in the aftermath of a disaster.
- America's high school graduation rate ranks nineteenth in the world.
- The United States is responsible for 25 percent of the carbon-dioxide emissions worldwide.
- People should get at least thirty minutes of exercise at least three days a week to improve their health.
- One million people in the United States live with AIDS; one-fourth are unaware of their condition.
- Over one billion people in the world live on less than one dollar a day.

Check out these websites for additional ideas:

http://www.volunteermatch.org
http://www.dosomething.org
http://www.getinvolved.gov

CONTRIBUTING TO COMMUNITY

Whether child abuse, world hunger, or saving the wetlands are your passion, get involved and get involved now. The benefits to your career and the world are endless.

Community Strategy #3: Ask for Help on HOW to Get Involved

Perhaps your challenge is not what to do but how to begin. This is where the meaningful relationships cultivated in Chapter 3 achieve additional value.

I recently received an e-mail from the Chief Financial Officer (CFO) at a growing company who feels ready for a new challenge and opportunity to make a difference in the community. Bryan is a classic Career Equity builder. He took the initiative to reach out to me and ask for help connecting with leaders of nonprofit organizations.

We brainstormed his interests in education, homelessness, and places that promote family interaction (example: the Zoo or Magic House) and where his talents and expertise in finance could be of value.

The next step was to identify people Bryan could network with to learn more about these organizations and their volunteer needs. Given Bryan's interest in children and education, I thought an introduction to the new president of De La Salle Middle School would be a good place to start. De La Salle's mission is to make high quality education accessible to underprivileged urban children. De La Salle is a growing organization and the Board could benefit from Bryan's financial acumen. We were able to schedule a meeting with the executive director and Board president. Bryan is now in the process of doing his "homework" and meeting with Board members to explore if this is the right place for his community contribution. Bryan knows that by taking initiative to serve others he will gain career assets through new experiences, learning, and relationships.

Community Strategy #4: Be Clear about Your Role
Like other dimensions of building Career Equity, Contributing to Community demands commitment. Once you find a place to volunteer, it is important to understand your role as a volunteer. There are numerous types of volunteer opportunities, but few places that prepare an individual for a volunteer experience. This lack of preparation often leads to inadequate volunteers and disappointment. Here are four key strategies for ensuring that your investment of time and talent reaps benefits for the organization and your career:

1) **Follow through on commitments.** If you inform an agency that you will be volunteering for them, follow through with your commitment. Nonprofit organizations and agencies rely heavily on the support of volunteers, and they make plans based on your promises.

2) **Show up on time.** Good volunteers show up on time. Employees of nonprofit organizations may be coordinating hundreds of different volunteers and schedules. It undermines the value of your gift if you disrupt their schedule and services.

CONTRIBUTING TO COMMUNITY

3) **Do what is asked.** Many times volunteer opportunities at nonprofit organizations aren't glamorous, but the role has importance. For example, the Humane Society needs volunteers to clean out cages or make follow-up phone calls to families who recently adopted a pet. Do your homework on the volunteer assignment upfront. Remember, at the end of the day, giving is about doing what is needed instead of what is wanted, expected, or planned.

4) **Communicate a positive spirit.** Just like in your career role, people love working with volunteers with a positive attitude who are happy to serve in whatever capacity they can. In addition, many nonprofits utilize long-term, enthusiastic volunteers for more complex tasks and projects. Volunteering that starts by simply stuffing envelopes often leads to larger more influential roles such as planning events, fundraisers, or being nominated to the Board of Directors.

5) **Define Your Giving Goals.** Like other dimensions of building Career Equity, you are more likely to achieve success and satisfaction if you have a plan and clear goals for your contribution. Every year when I set my business goals, I define and document my community contribution goals in specific and measurable terms. As I mentioned earlier, playing a role in organizing a successful *Purses for Pooches* event is one of my giving goals. I set a specific personal financial contribution, investment of time, and goal for growing the number of women who will learn about the Humane Society's mission.

After each event I assess the level of our goal achievement and begin thinking about how to increase it for the following year. I know that using this discipline for me and for the committee has yielded double-digit growth of "friend and fund raising" every year for the past five years. What are your goals for giving this year?

6) **Invite Others and Expand the Envelope.** I was recently invited to play golf in the annual "Scramble for Kids" golf tournament sponsored by The Qualy Group of Northwestern Mutual Financial Network. John Qualy is a role model of "contributing to community." His generosity is not an occasional event. It comes from his heart and permeates every aspect of his personal and professional life. The "Scramble for Kids" raises about $100,000 each year for the Children's Miracle Network (CMN). Most importantly, John's leadership in organizing this event teaches others about the value of showing up and giving. This is a relationship-enhancing day. John's best financial representatives invite clients and friends to join them on the course. After eighteen holes of golf, it is hard not to make new personal and professional connections. Who invites you to participate in important giving events? Are you showing up? Do you invite others to participate? Taking initiative to invite others to your special events communicates that you care about them and believe in the multiplier effect of introducing colleagues to a worthy cause.

CONTRIBUTING TO COMMUNITY

Which of the six community strategies is a strength for you? Which one is most interesting? As we will explore in Chapter 7, Career Equity is built through strategic action. Pick one area of "contributing to community" and take one small action today.

Extra Credit:

1) Check out the United Way's web site at http://www.liveunited.org/.
2) Read Claire Gualdoini, *The Greater Good: How Philanthropy Drives the American Economy and Can Save Capitalism* (New York: Times Books, 2003).
3) Ask your Career Board of Directors about where they gave and how you can make a difference.

6: Reaping the Right Recognition and Rewards

"In the arena of human life the honors and rewards fall to those who show their good qualities in action."

—Aristotle

Reaping the Right Recognition and Rewards is the final asset of building Career Equity. This element is last because recognition and reward are outcomes of managing, building, and cultivating a purposeful career.

A recent Towers Watson Global Workforce Study (2010) of more than 20,000 employees in mid-size to large companies across 22 industries reveals that competitive base pay and vacation or paid time off are among the top five career-attractiveness factors for all employees and in the top two for employees in Generation Y (Gen Y). Yet, all too often, professionals are too passive when it comes to managing salary and benefits.

Think for a moment about when you accepted your current position. Did you negotiate for a higher salary or benefits? In other words, if your employer offered $70,000 in base salary, did you ask for $75,000 or a $10,000 signing bonus or more time off? If you did, you were consciously building Career Equity. You are also in the minority. This is a Career Equity paradox. While recognition and reward are among the important and meaningful assets, many professionals do not take the initiative to understand or ask for the recognition and rewards available or that they deserve.

This lack of awareness, combined with a reluctance to ask for greater rewards, often leads to regret. When we discover peers are more effective at researching, articulating needs, and delivering results that reap greater rewards, we can be frustrated and disappointed. Purposeful management of this asset is needed to avoid the risk of leaving significant opportunities on the table.

In their widely acclaimed book *Women Don't Ask*, Dr. Linda Babcock and Dr. Sarah Laschever illustrate the consequences for failing to manage our rewards and recognition. Their reserach reveals the compounded loss of a $5,000 difference in salary over a 30-year career. In other words, by failing to ask at the start of a career, one could lose nearly $400,000 in income. This does not take into account the compounding effect of money or of later promotions and progressions. While Dr. Babcock's and Dr. Laschever's research is a wake-up call to women, it is also compelling to men. While men are better at asking initially, a significant number leave money "on the table," too, and are not negotiating for the right rewards.

We have been focusing on the reward of a competitive base salary. While this asset is a forceful factor of career growth, there are other forms of recognition and reward which are ignored and undervalued. Career assets of tuition reimbursement, disability insurance, wellness programs and fitness memberships, are just a few examples.

The critical first step of reaping the right recognition and rewards is to understand the array of rewards available and how your chosen career aligns to these options. With the accessibility of information through the Internet there is no excuse for a lack of awareness. Below are three proven resources used by Career Equity builders to conduct due diligence about career rewards:

I. Salary.com (http://www.salary.com/)
Salary.com is all about compensation. This web site offers personalized salary reports, articles, and surveys. Salary.com tools gives you a clear perspective on what employers are paying based on job title, location, experience level, and education.

II. Payscale (http://www.payscale.com/)
Payscale provides compensation information for employers and individuals. This resource has thousands of profiles in their database. Users get free comparison reports with compensation ranges, common benefits, and job opportunities.

III. GlassDoor (http://www.glassdoor.com/)
GlassDoor is a career community that enables job seekers to see employee opinions about a company's work environment along with details of pay and benefits. It also has CEO approval rat-

ings and recently launched a new section that includes reviews of job interviews.

In addition, professional associations also frequently conduct salary surveys for their membership. This is yet another way that your active involvement in a professional group can help you build Career Equity.

Let's refer back to Career Asset #5—**Reaping the Right Rewards & Recognition in the Career Equity Assessment**. (See page 77). Where do you see gaps in your reward and recognition account? With a little planning and sense of purpose you can increase your return on this career investment.

How much time have you spent in the last year investigating pay, recognition, or benefits in your current or desired career? Are you fully utilizing the resources available to you? Here are five best practices you can employ to achieve greater rewards.

Five Ways to Reap Greater Rewards
1) **Conduct research or career due diligence first.** As mentioned, previously researching salaries, benefits, and potential rewards comparable to your chosen role before you attend an interview or participate in a performance review is critical. Know where the high, median, and low salaries are for someone with your skills, experience, and education. Don't assume that salary and/or benefits aren't negotiable. Remember that benefits can equal up to 25 percent of any employment package. Negotiating salary prior to having a

REAPING THE RIGHT RECOGNITION AND REWARDS

Career Asset #5 The Right Rewards and Recognition	Scale of 1–5
In the past month, I received recognition or praise for my work	
I know the market value of pay and benefits for my position and experience	
I use at least 70% or more of my vacation time annually	
I participate in a 401K program or other retirement savings plan	
I am fully informed about my health care benefits; medical, dental, life insurance, long-term disability	
I am satisfied with my level of compensation – base pay	
I have a high degree of flexibility in choosing when I take time off for vacation, etc.	
My organization makes contributions to charities or organizations I believe in	
The people I work with want me to succeed and advance	
In the past month, I have given recognition or praise to a co-worker	
Total Points for This Asset (50 possible)	

detailed understanding of a company's benefit package may prove costly. Research reveals that the majority of employers expect you to negotiate. Many consider it a test of assertiveness and initiative.

2) Consider the whole package. Remember to add benefits such as educational reimbursements, vacation time, and travel allowances into your negotiations. These are elements of your entire reward package and are often overlooked. Don't get hung up on base salary. Benefits that make your life easier, increase skill sets, or save you time accelerate Career Equity and may be easy for your employer to implement too. Doing your rewards homework on the whole package also speaks volumes about you. It says you manage from facts; you are purposeful about your career, and have the courage to seek a win-win. If you have worked in one firm for several years, now may be a good time to review your company benefit options. Schedule a time to speak with a Human Resources professional to get an update. In today's dynamic business environment, rewards change quickly. Being informed is a key step to accumulating greater career wealth.

3) Stay with the pulse of your industry. Make sure that your skills, experience, and education are properly aligned with your discipline. This is further evidence for the importance of Career Equity Asset #3—Relentless Pursuit of Learning and Growth. Continually reading about trends in your industry keeps you on the leading edge and prepared for conversations with colleagues and leaders. For example, if a major supplier is expanding and growing, how can your company cross sell new services? One of our clients works with WalMart. By staying on top of industry trends, our client recognized the opportunity to expand their services to other national retailers (e.g., Target, Kohl's, etc.). The reward: The client's team now has a new division focused on national retailing and the individual who identified the opportunity has greater Career Equity—he is leading the group.

4) **Point out your value and seek a win-win.** When negotiating rewards and recognition, discuss how you can contribute to the organization's desired results and not simply what you want. Providing concrete examples of how your skills and contributions support the company's goals increase the probability of achieving mutual value. For example, one professional was able to demonstrate how his networking at a professional organization led to recruitment of three new sales reps. Another professional made the correlation between the presentation and how it resulted in bringing a new client to the firm. In both cases, the initiative and activity achieved a result.

As one my client's is fond of saying, "leadership is defined by results." While employers value effort, they pay for results. Keep track of results you are achieving so you

BUILDING CAREER EQUITY

can make a compelling case for win-win rewards. Never make one-sided reward requests focused exclusively on your needs. Leaders don't want to hear that you are behind on your mortgage or have kids going to college. Leave personal needs out of negotiations.

5) Give often. Another positive Career Equity paradox paradox is that giving leads to more rewards. Teach a class, mentor someone, or give your knowledge away. When I read a compelling article, I send it to clients and colleagues I think will benefit from the information. I also publish a quarterly e-newsletter to provide colleagues and clients with best practices, new books, tools, or resources that advance their goals. In addition to the intrinsic satisfaction of helping others, this sharing has resulted in new members to my CEO Book Club, new clients, and opportunities to speak at a national organization. Here are a few examples of how to give that make your career experience richer and more rewarding:

- Volunteer to be a coach or "go to person" for a new member of the firm or project team.
- Offer to take notes at a team meeting or learning conference and publish the summary for other team members.
- Organize a community event such as a "fund-raiser" for the United Way or another cause of interest.
- Send a note of appreciation to firm leaders for spon-

REAPING THE RIGHT RECOGNITION AND REWARDS

soring a fun event. Note: you would be amazed how few professionals acknowledge these efforts and how much they are valued by the leaders who rarely receive positive upward feedback.

What are you giving away? All of these career rewards and recognition are a function of giving ideas and knowledge to others. Take a few minutes and brainstorm giving ideas that are relevant and energizing to you or your organization. Then pick one and put it into action.

Managing the whole package of rewards and benefits is critical to optimize Career Equity. But let's explore three often mismanaged or disregarded benefits: 1) employer-sponsored savings, 2) paid time off, and 3) health care benefits. A quick examination of these reward options may uncover unrealized benefits in your career portfolio.

Investing in Your Future Now—Contributing to a 401K

When I was starting my career at McDonnell Douglas Corp., the company matched every dollar I saved in the 401K program with stock. In other words, if I saved one dollar, they would deposit a dollar of stock in my retirement account. As an HR professional, I had access to reports of employee participation in this program. Less than 30 percent of all employees who had the option to participate did.

BUILDING CAREER EQUITY

When I left the organization seven years later, McDonnell Douglas was sold to The Boeing Company and the stock had split three times during my tenure. In other words, I left with three times the stock I had contributed.

What was even more amazing is that when I went to Arthur Andersen, I found the same thing. I assumed that smart financially driven CPAs would understand the value of compounded savings. Again, only 34 percent participated in the firm's 401K program. This is not isolated to big firms or companies. The current financial crisis has highlighted the cost of poor savings habits. In the United States, the individual savings rate is only about four percent up from one percent in the last five years. Career Equity builders are not satisfied with these results. They want to fully utilize every tool at their disposal to increase tangible and intangible rewards.

Investigate the savings options available to you today. Many organizations have an intranet with a description of employee benefits. Take the initiative to meet with Human Resources professionals. Either way, find out what savings options are available to you and begin or increase your contribution. The smallest amount invested today yields great Career Equity in the future. Also, when you leave or change jobs don't forget to "roll-over" these investments. Seek the guidance of a financial services advisor to explore how the equity you have built can be accumulated and combined with equity you will accumulate in your new role or company.

The Reward of Paid Time Off—Are You Taking It?

Let's examine another reward that is often underappreciated: vacation or paid time off. According to a *New York Times'* "Vacation Deprivation" survey, many Americans do not use all of their paid time away from work. The survey reveals that on average, workers will likely lose up to three days of vacation time this year.

Additionally, according to the findings of a survey by travel site Expedia.com of 1,301 workers, employers get about 415 million vacation days returned to them. Even those that do use their vacation time say that they are checking their e-mail or office voice mail while they are off. Nearly one-third (32 percent) say they work while on vacation. The average vacation allotment for the workers was 12.4 days a year. Losing two to three days a year over a 20-year career is nearly two months of pay. If someone offered you two months of free pay would you take it? More importantly, unplugging from work on a regular basis has been shown to increase energy, creativity, and outlook about work.

Health Care Bane or Benefit?

In an affluent culture like the United States, employer-paid health care has become a career entitlement. The high cost of health care combined with broad changes in health care reform will undoubtedly change the valence or level of importance of this Career Equity factor in years to come.

According to the 2006 Employer Health Benefits Survey released by the Kaiser Family Foundation, health care premiums increased more than twice as fast as workers' wages and overall inflation. In 2009, the average annual premiums for employer-sponsored health insurance were $4,824 for single coverage and $13,375 for family coverage. Premiums for family coverage are five percent higher last year ($12,680). Since 1999, average premiums for family coverage have increased 131 percent. "Working people don't feel like they are getting any relief because their premiums have been rising faster than their paychecks," says Foundation President and CEO Drew Altman.

Being informed and engaged with your health care benefits enhances Career Equity. How much does your employer plan save you? Do you fully understand COBRA benefits if your career exit is unplanned (e.g., layoff)? Take the time to review health care options and the cost of premiums to you and your employer.

The Right Recognition

Is receiving recognition important to you? A Harris poll asked, "What two or three things do you want most in a job?" "Recognition for a job well done" was in the top three. Additionally, in a recent *Workforce* article, Bob Nelson, a nationally known recognition guru, says "More than anything else, employees want to be valued for a job well done by those they hold in high esteem."

REAPING THE RIGHT RECOGNITION AND REWARDS

While we highly value recognition, most professionals are not proactive in getting it. Rather, it can seem arbitrary and outside of our control. To increase the thoughtful recognition you receive you must model the behavior you want. Mahatma Gandhi's wisdom is relevant here: "Be the change you want to see in the world." When was the last time you recognized a peer or colleague for a job well done? How do you feel when you express appreciation in a sincere and thoughtful way? Giving meaningful recognition has an immediate intrinsic benefit to you and the receiver. As with many dimensions of Career Equity it results in mutual growth. Here are a few recognition practices that deliver the right rewards:

1) **Develop a weekly discipline of writing one handwritten note of appreciation to someone.** In our high-tech world, high-touch habits such as note writing have diminished. How many times have you kept a handwritten note or card someone sent you? In my experience, they are superior to e-mail. Cultivating this discipline improves positive proactive communication and builds meaningful relationships.

2) **Research award and recognition traditions in your company or community and go for one.** Awards and incentive programs are designed to highlight behaviors that matter most to company results. Company leaders have a defined win-win in these programs. For example, the Barry Wehm-

iller organization awards the use of a company Chevrolet SSR for a week to an employee who is nominated by peers for exceptional performance. Winning these awards can be fun, engage peers, and depending on their significance, can differentiate you from others. For example, in the financial-security industry, the Million Dollar Round Table (MDRT) is earned by fewer than 10 percent of all financial services professionals. Once achieved it is recognition with meaning to the individual, their clients, and their income.

Many professionals ask me how to gain recognition awarded by local business journals (e.g., Most Influential Business Women, or Top 30 Under 30, or Fastest Growing Firm award, etc.). First, know the criteria for the award and determine its relevance to your skills, talents, and aspirations. Second, apply or ask someone to nominate you and do so in a timely manner. You would be amazed at the number of people who are not eligible because they don't meet the deadline. Provide nominators with background information as needed. Third, follow-up to ensure all relevant information is received. Send notes of congratulations to those who receive the award, even if you don't. Don't forget to recognize the people who contributed to your success. Few, if any of us achieve great results alone.

The purpose of this chapter is to optimize the recognition and rewards most compelling to you. Career Equity builders know what motivates them. They are informed about the pay,

REAPING THE RIGHT RECOGNITION AND REWARDS

benefits, and perquisites (tangible or intangible) and achieve them with intention and purpose.

Recently, I received an email from a professional who is very purposeful about enhancing her tangible recognition and rewards. She is a development director (internal coach) to financial advisors. She works hard to develop and provide them with systems, tools, and challenging feedback to achieve their business goals. She had the feeling that her work was not realizing rewards comparable to other leaders in her role. We discussed a plan for her to research peer compensation, the rewards she wanted, and the impact her work has on business results. In other words, she needed to know, in specific terms, how helping financial advisors achieve a greater percentage of their goals benefited the managing director's revenue.

After our interaction, she completed a thorough review of peer rewards and the organization's results. She sent me an analysis of these factors and solicited my feedback; to give her another perspective (a great example of how to use a mentor or accountability advisor in the process). After we discussed a few changes, we did a role play of how she would present her findings and recommendations to the managing director. The next step was to schedule a meeting with the managing director, present her feelings and findings, and solicit his feedback. Remember achieving the right recognition and rewards is about finding the win-win. She needed to articulate her needs in a way that demonstrated how the organization profits when she gets the rewards she wants. Her story illustrates what Career Equity building is all about. She identified gaps in her career satisfaction, researched the facts, organized a solution, and solicited feedback from mentors or experienced leaders to improve her solution. I'm confident that her approach will yield an increase in her compensation. Most importantly, it increases the intangible asset of empowering herself to articulate her needs and see an improved result.

Where can you gain greater reward and recognition for your career contributions?

Would taking some well-earned time off, investing in your firm's sponsored 401K, or negotiating a pay increase take your career satisfaction to the next level? Pick one area that would create a great return on your investment, and like the Nike slogan says, "Just Do It."

Extra Credit:

1) Read Linda Babcock and Sarah Laschever *Women Don't Ask: Negotiation and the Gender Divide* (Princeton, NJ: Princeton University Press, 2003).
2) Check out—Arthur D. Rosenberg *101 Ways to Stand Out at Work: How to Get the Recognition and Rewards You Deserve* (Avon, MA: Adams Media and F+W Media Company, 2009).
3) Nominate a colleague for a special recognition in your firm or community.

7: Putting Action and Accountability Behind Aspirations

"The Common Denominator of Success—the secret of success of every person who has ever been successful—lies in the fact that they formed the habit of doing things that failures don't like to do."

—Albert E.N. Gray

Great rewards await those who define goals and act purposefully to achieve them. In addition to the intrinsic value of achieving something significant, David Kohl, professor emeritus at Virginia Tech., found that people who regularly write down their goals earn nine times more income over their lifetimes than people who don't.

Unfortunately, Kohl's research also reveals a disturbing fact. Eighty percent (80%) of Americans say they don't have goals. Sixteen percent do have goals, but don't write them down and less than four percent write down their goals. Only one percent of Americans review their goals on regular basis.

If you are investing the time and resources to read this book you are clearly in the top 20 percent. You have goals and aspirations. The question is whether you will choose to be in the top four or even one percent of professionals who commit their goals to writing and review them regularly.

BUILDING CAREER EQUITY

The purpose of this chapter is to equip you with the tools to put your career aspirations into action. My passion and purpose is to help leaders achieve significant results, not just identify them. Through my work with leaders from the nation's best firms, I have gained a unique perspective on what differentiates those who achieve bold goals in their business, career, and life from those who don't.

On the surface it is deceptively simple. However, like most noteworthy efforts, it demands something extra. The important thing to know is that this capacity is learned and can be taught to others.

While the focus of this book is on career building, these habits are transferrable to other areas of life (e.g., spiritual, physical, etc.). As Kohl's research reveals, those who achieve abundance foster a habit of thinking about their aspirations daily. They relentlessly keep score of their progress. What does your goal setting and review discipline reveal today?

How often do you think about these goals? What accountability do you have in place to act on them—every day?

To convert your career aspirations into reality you need to create and sustain four goal-achievement habits:

Habit #1 – Get Organized. Create a place where all of your career goals, ideas, and action plans are kept. If it sounds fundamental, it is. I see business leader's every day that have piles of forms, goals, and ideas but lack the organization to move goals forward quickly.

PUTTING ACTION AND ACCOUNTABILITY BEHIND ASPIRATIONS

Organize a written document which includes your "vital" career goals and plans for the next year. Be as creative and imaginative as you want. Some professionals use pictures and images with written goals to help them "see" their ultimate success. The critical element of this habit is to ensure the goals are measurable and achievable and kept in a location where you will review the goals frequently. I have a one-page description of my annual goals in a notebook I carry with me daily.

I mention "vital" goals. Fewer than seven is ideal. It is difficult to work on more than seven goals concurrently and achieve significance. Less in goal setting is truly more. The following is an example of a well-defined goal:

After assessing his Career Equity in Asset 3, relentless Learning and Growth, Bob set a goal to achieve a Chartered Financial Analyst (CFA) accreditation by December of 2011.

The goal is specific, measurable, achievable, and time-oriented: all elements of an effective career goal. Most importantly it aligns with Bob's assessment and aspiration to build more Career Equity in Learning and Growth.

Habit #2 – Convert Long-Term Goals to Short-Term Action Steps. While we love thinking of long-term dreams or aspirations, it is action that turns goals into reality. The following commonly held professional achievement illustrates the point. Graduating from college is a long-term career aspiration that requires a minimum of four and up to ten years (if you pursue a PhD or medical degree) to achieve. To earn a "walk across the stage" and receive a college diploma demands hundreds, if not thousands, of action steps.

If we attended to all those steps when we began, we would be overwhelmed and never complete our goal. This may be why, according to the 2000 U.S. Census, that only 15.5 percent of adults succeed in achieving a bachelor's degree and less than nine percent graduate with a masters or PhD. Those who succeed learn how to focus their time and attention on actions required in the present. For example, each semester you want to attend college you must register for courses. If you were intent and organized in this process, you typically got the courses you wanted at the time of day and with the professor you preferred. If you procrastinated and did not follow a purposeful action plan, it is likely your class schedule was less than ideal. The difference demonstrates the impact of actions on purpose or those taken by accident. With simple planning and action we can optimize our life and performance.

Let's apply this insight to building equity in your career portfolio today.

Let's say you want to enhance a relationship with a leader or mentor in your organization and build more equity by cultivating meaningful relationships.

Your action plan might look like the chart on page 93:

PUTTING ACTION AND ACCOUNTABILITY BEHIND ASPIRATIONS

Goal, Aspiration, or Desired Result	Actions	By When	Status
Build a stronger relationship with ...	1. Schedule a meeting with:	No later than Sept. 30th	
	2. Prepare several questions or issues I want feedback on during our meeting	September 15th	
	3. Make reservations for lunch at restaurant	September 18th	
	4. Send follow-up note or thank-you for their time	Day after lunch	
	5. Send a status note on issues we discussed and how I have acted on their feedback	30 days after lunch	

How long do you think it took to define this action plan? Answer: About 10 to 15 minutes to organize. I share this because often the first response to organizing is "I don't have time for that." We spend more energy fighting against a new habit or discipline than simply doing it.

Take ten minutes to organize your actions and see how you feel when the plan is outlined.

The action plan above contains specific, deadline driven, realistic steps that can be achieved in the timeframe outlined. A great deal is written on how to create action plans. You can surf the web for various strategies. Discover the approach that works best for you. The most essential step is to write them down and put them with your career portfolio where you can find them and review them easily.

Habit #3 – Develop a Systematic Review of Goals and Results. The third and most important habit to form is the systematic review of goals and results. This is what separates good goal achievers from great goal achievers. Human behavior often works against consistent, relentless effort. We love the next new thing, idea, and so on. As Professor Kohl's research reveals less than one percent of people review their goals on a consistent basis. Why is this so rare? Because systematically reviewing an action plan demands self-discipline and the ability to confront disappointment. While writing a well-defined action plan increases the probability of achieving our goals, the

PUTTING ACTION AND ACCOUNTABILITY BEHIND ASPIRATIONS

regular and consistent review keeps us focused, honest, and disturbed when we are not progressing.

The tension that occurs when we realize actions not taken is the fuel or motivation to get us back on track. Those who build high Career Equity and accomplish significant goals have the courage to confront the gap between what they said they would do (aspiration) and what they are doing (reality).

Here is an ideal review schedule and checklist:

Monthly – Schedule about thirty minutes each month to review all of your annual goals and Vision or Three-Year Letter. Check in on how your aspirations are progressing and identify the things that need action in the next thirty days.

Weekly – Create another thirty-minute investment of time to align the week ahead to monthly actions. Like a chiropractor making small adjustments, you will achieve big positive changes in the long term for honoring this discipline. For example, if one of your monthly goals is to attend a professional credential workshop. Decide what can be done this week to advance that goal. Can I submit the registration form this week or review the pre-work materials? When I do my weekly planning on Sunday evenings, I pull out my schedule for the week ahead and my goals and ask myself the following questions:

When this week is over, what will I feel great about achieving? What would make me feel that I have used my time effectively and advanced some part of my longer-term aspirations? I have a one-page form where I record my "Desired Results" for the week and check several times a week to track my progress and reconcile accomplished goals with those not met.

Here are a few examples of what you would see on my weekly Desired Results list:

- Write a one-page case study on goal achievement for clients and post on web site
- Exercise aerobically 3x and practice yoga on Saturday
- Document a client-strategic plan and send to the leadership team.

Daily – Spend five to ten minutes at the beginning of each day creating a "To Do" list. The art and science of this action and accountability tool is to ensure the other two review habits are implemented. Many people generate a "To Do" list in isolation. Without a context for longer-term aspirations, a "To Do" list can be an energy vampire.

Those who systematically review their goals monthly, weekly, and daily have high Career Equity, are extremely satisfied, and often arrive at aspirations ahead of schedule. If all of these tools leave you feeling overwhelmed, don't avoid the accountability. Pick one habit that is most relevant and try it for the next thirty days.

PUTTING ACTION AND ACCOUNTABILITY BEHIND ASPIRATIONS

Habit #4 – Invoke Accountability Advisors. The fourth and final habit is to cultivate the practice of asking for accountability from those who want you to succeed. This habit is often more difficult than it sounds for independent goal achievement professionals. Yet, the rewards are exponential. Who in your life holds you accountable for realizing your goals and being the best version of yourself? Who has the courage to give you feedback about what you need to do differently?

Maggie's aspiration to grow a Family Office in the Wealth Management practice of one of the nation's top accounting firms is another example of the value of invoking accountability advisors. Maggie has a clear set of written goals and works hard to achieve them. She found her plan gained momentum when she asked to work with a leadership coach and asked the partners she worked with for a monthly meeting.

The operative word here is "asked." As Nathaniel Branden, internationally known author of the *Six Pillars of Self-Esteem* writes, "No one is coming to save you."

Career Equity builders, like Maggie, take the initiative to ask for support and accountability. The "ask" is not a sign of weakness, but a reflection of strength and clarity for personal and professional growth. This is not a strategy to get others to do your work for you. It is your work and career goals supported by those who want you to succeed. I put this habit last because it is most effective when the first three habits are in place. When you are organized, have specific action plans, and systematically review your goals, your request to others can be energizing for them and you. You will be specific about what you want and what you need to succeed. Maggie used her quarterly coaching meetings as a way to get new ideas about how to build her practice and develop her team. Then she would share the action plans she developed in her monthly partner meetings. This provided another mechanism of feedback and support.

Maggie's level of thinking and planning for reciprocal growth and results delighted the partners. They knew that when Maggie's goals were achieved, their practice and the firm would benefit, too. Because Maggie had a vision of what she wanted to achieve, organized her actions, and took the initiative to seek their feedback, the partners were eager to meet with her. They knew she wouldn't waste her time or theirs. They made introductions to their existing clients promoting Maggie's new service. Maggie is reaping the rewards of this accountability and support. Her practice has doubled in clients and revenue and she is doing more of the work she enjoys. Who would benefit from knowing about your goals? When will you take the initiative to ask for the added accountability to make your career goals a reality?

I want to close this chapter on action and accountability with an excerpt from *The Common Denominator of Success* written by Albert E. N. Gray. It was part of his address in 1940 to the National Life Underwriter's Association at their annual convention in Philadelphia.

PUTTING ACTION AND ACCOUNTABILITY BEHIND ASPIRATIONS

This speech is avidly read by the best professionals in the financial-security business today. Gray's insights about what differentiates goal achievers are relevant to any professional, in any organization, and any time:

"Any resolution or decision you make is simply a promise to you. It isn't worth a tinker's dam unless you have formed the habit of making it and keeping it. And you won't form the habit of making it and keeping it unless right at the start you link it with a definite purpose that can be accomplished by keeping it. In other words, any resolution or decision you make today has to be made again tomorrow, and the next day, and the next, and the next, and so on. And it not only has to be made each day, but it has to be kept each day, for if you miss one day in the making or keeping of it, you've got to go back and begin all over again. But if you continue the process of making it each morning and keeping it each day, you will finally wake up some morning a different person in a different world, and you will wonder what has happened to you and the world you used to live in."

Extra Credit

1) Read David Allen, *Getting Things Done* (New York: Penguin Group, 2001).
2) Read Albert E. N. Gray, *The New Common Denominator of Success* (Albany, Oregon: May 2008).
2) Organize a time to do weekly planning for thirty minutes.

8: Cultivating a Career Equity Culture

"Someone's sitting in the shade today because someone planted a tree a long time ago."
—Warren Buffett

Dear Firm Leader or Manager,

If you are reading this, I know you have a desire to build an organization that provides professionals with a unique and meaningful career experience. You understand the connection between professional growth/retention and organizational performance. Most importantly, you believe that creating an organizational culture demands a clear purpose and relentless implementation of proven practices.

This chapter is written exclusively for leaders like you who desire, know, and believe that mutually beneficial relationships with professionals are superior. While professionals can and will benefit from mastering the Career Equity model individually, exponential growth comes from implementing these practices organizationally. This chapter provides you with proven practices and disciplines needed to cultivate a Career Equity Culture. A culture that attracts and most importantly retains the best talent for your organization requires different ways of thinking and communicating. Many of your peers don't know about these practices. At least their behavior does not reflect that they do.

However, an enlightened set of the nation's best professional firms have implemented the Career Equity philosophy systematically and are reaping the rewards. They achieve a greater market share of the best recruits and their average tenure of the best professionals exceeds competitors by more than two years. They have also recognized a measurable increase in profitability. You are also likely to find them on "The Best Places to Work" lists. Would you like your firm to realize greater results in these areas?

If you are like most leaders, you have heard and read the statistics. You know that the average tenure of professional talent is about 2.5 years and that profitability drops when the recruiting, training, and development investments you make walk out the door for greener pastures. A recent global workforce study, conducted by Towers Watson (2010) found that more than 89 percent of employees believe career management is their responsibility, but only about 30 percent get adequate support from managers to realize their aspirations. More alarming is that nearly 60 percent consult their peers when making a decision to stay or go. Peers are not the folks you want guiding career choices of top performers alone.

Let's take a look at the way you collaborate with professionals. What percentage of the people in your organization consider you or one of your leaders a trusted career advisor?

How many would be the first to tell you if they received an offer from one of your competitors? What mechanisms are in place to have purposeful conversations about each professional's career vision?

The road map for creating such a place is here.
The first step to cultivating a Career Equity culture requires knowing what matters most for each professional. This means having a planned and intentional career discussion with every person in your company or firm. This is not an annual performance review. Understanding the career goals and aspirations of the people important to your enterprise demands more than a meeting once a year. This conversation begins in the recruiting process and persists throughout a professional's work in your firm. On average, leaders who are reaping the rewards of a Career Equity culture meet with professionals four times a year to check in on career goals, achievement, and satisfaction. However, they don't get hung up on the frequency of meetings. They know that the most important thing is to understand, in explicit terms, what energizes each professional. Further, they are relentless about ensuring professionals have the right relationships to support career achievement.

Here is an example of the types of questions that get a thoughtful career conversation started in the recruiting process; many are relevant for career conversations after professionals are onboard:

BUILDING CAREER EQUITY

- Tell me about your career experience to this point. What are the two to three things that you enjoy most about your work? What two to three things are not as energizing for you in this role?
- Our business is all about client service. Our people are professionals that value serving and pleasing clients. If I were to contact a few of your clients what would they say are your two or three strengths? In other words, why do they work with you?
- What would your managers or partners say are your two or three areas for growth and development?
- What achievement in your career are you most proud of and why?
- Tell me about a time, you had to serve leaders who had competing needs or demands. How did you resolve the conflict of time/resources?
- Tell me about a time, when you had to take the lead in a new function or team. What challenges did you confront in this new role? How did you overcome them?
- What brings you the greatest sense of satisfaction in your work?

Leaders who realize great results in recruitment and retention use the five Career Equity components as a framework for delivering compelling career practices consistently. For example, one of the nation's top engineering firms realized a

20 percent increase in retention by integrating Career Equity elements into their performance management system and ensuring every professional has a "trusted advisor" to consult about significant career choices.

Like Chapter 1, where each professional is invited to assess his or her current level of career effectiveness, the best place for leaders to begin building a Career Equity culture is to assess how the organization is providing professionals with the resources to cultivate and grow their careers. The following Career Equity Culture Assessment will help you and your leaders identify firm strengths and places for optimizing career development strategies. The actual numbers are less important than the awareness and alignment that is derived from having a purposeful conversation about the firm's culture.

Tool: Career Equity Culture Assessment: Using a scale where 10 = very true of our firm's practices today, 5 = somewhat true of our firm today, and 1 = not at all true of our organization's career practices today, read each of the statements and place the appropriate rating in the box to the right of the statement.

Creating a Career Equity Culture is achieved over time and with systematic attention to the growth and development of each professional. Guidelines on page 111 will help you evaluate your organization's current level of effectiveness.

BUILDING CAREER EQUITY

This component of the assessment measures the extent to which the firm is Providing Engaging Work for professionals. After completing an individual assessment, compare the results with other partners, associates, and/or Human Resource leaders. What patterns and trends emerge from an integrated assessment of the firm's current state?

Career Asset #1 Providing Engaging Work	Scale of 1 – 10
1. We know the career vision of every professional in our firm, and they are written for future reference	
2. Each professional has a measurable set of goals for things that are most important to accomplish, and this is reviewed on a regular basis with a firm leader or manager	
3. Each professional's work reflects a high degree of autonomy and independence	
4. We measure the career satisfaction of every professional in a systematic way	
5. Our recruitment practices intentionally measure the fit between candidate career aspirations and the needs of our organization	
Total Points for This Asset (50 possible)	

Notes, observations, and questions that emerged as you completed the assessment:

CULTIVATING A CAREER EQUITY CULTURE

This component of the assessment measures the extent to which the firm provides opportunities for Cultivating Meaningful Relationships. After completing an individual assessment, compare the results with other partners, associates, and/or Human Resource leaders. What patterns and trends emerge from an integrated assessment of the firm's current state?

Career Asset #2 Cultivating Meaningful Relationships	Scale of 1 – 10
1. We know the names of each professional's mentors or career advisors in our company or firm	
2. We coach professionals to build an effective network of colleagues, inside and outside the firm	
3. We have a system or practice for soliciting feedback from each professional about how to improve mentor relationships in our firm	
4. Our mentors or career advisors meet with professionals, at least quarterly, on an individual basis	
5. Mentors and career advisors receive specific training and skill development	
Total Points for This Asset (50 possible)	

Notes, observations, and questions that emerged as you completed the assessment:

This component of the assessment measures the extent to which the firm provides opportunities for Learning and Professional Growth. After completing an individual assessment, compare the results with other partners, associates, and/or Human Resource leaders. What patterns and trends emerge from an integrated assessment of the firm's current state?

Career Asset #3 Learning & Professional Growth	Scale of 1 – 10
1. Each professional has a formal learning, growth, and development plan with specific measurable goals	
2. Professionals are encouraged to teach or facilitate training/learning programs at least once a year	
3. Our performance management system requires each professional to complete a self-evaluation	
4. There is an intentional link between career goals and work assignments/projects	
5. Department or company training budgets are allocated to ensure the best professionals are receiving the right learning and growth and reviewed for implementation regularly	
Total Points for This Asset (50 possible)	

Notes, observations, and questions that emerged as you completed the assessment:

CULTIVATING A CAREER EQUITY CULTURE

This component of the assessment measures the extent to which the firm provides opportunities for Contributing to Community. After completing an individual assessment, compare the results with other partners, associates, and/or Human Resource leaders. What patterns and trends emerge from an integrated assessment of the firm's current state?

Career Asset #4 Contributing to Community	Scale of 1 – 10
1. Our organization promotes the success of civic and nonprofit organizations (events, donations, etc.)	
2. We provide time away from work for our professionals to participate in "giving back" (e.g., Habit for Humanity building project)	
3. We have written "giving goals" for the company and encourage professionals to set individual goals	
4. Our organization has a positive reputation in the community for giving and contributing	
5. Our leaders serve on boards or committees of not-for-profit organizations in our community	
Total Points for This Asset (50 possible)	

Notes, observations, and questions that emerged as you completed the assessment:

BUILDING CAREER EQUITY

This component of the assessment measures the extent to which the firm provides The Right Recognition & Rewards. After completing an individual assessment, compare the results with other partners, associates, and/or Human Resource leaders. What patterns and trends emerge from an integrated assessment of the firm's current state?

Career Asset #5 The Right Recognition & Rewards	Scale of 1 – 10
1. We teach leaders and mentors how to make recognition and praise personal and meaningful	
2. We provide our professionals with tools to evaluate the market value of pay and benefits compared to competitors	
3. Professionals have a high degree of autonomy in scheduling vacations and are encouraged by firm leaders to use it	
4. We offer a 401K program and it has nearly 80 percent participation	
5. Our Firm provides comprehensive health care coverage; medical, dental, life insurance, and long-term disability	
Total Points for This Asset (50 possible)	

Notes, observations, and questions that emerged as you completed the assessment:

CULTIVATING A CAREER EQUITY CULTURE

Evaluation Guidelines

- Scores between 45 and 50, in a category indicate exceptional investment and commitment to professional career growth. The firm has a competitive advantage in this area.

- Scores that fall between 35 and 44 in a category indicate intentional effort and energy are in place to accelerate professional career success. The firm enjoys several best practices in this area.

- Scores that fall between 25 and 34 in a category indicate a moderate level of attention is given to helping professionals advance career growth. The firm would benefit from a higher level of leadership focus and commitment to career development strategies.

- Any category total of 24 or less indicates a need for attention and an actionable plan.

While having exceptional scores in every area is desirable, it is not typical. Organizations purposeful about creating a Career Equity Culture over the long-term will focus on the vital few areas where improvement is needed and work to do so!

After reviewing your scores in each area, what stands out to you about the current state of your Career Equity culture? Which of the assets yielded the highest number of points? Which asset has the fewest number of points?

Cultivating a culture of career growth demands purposeful processes and behavior. Cynicism is alive and well in organizations today because many leaders say that people and career growth are "their most important asset" and then behave in ways that are incongruent with this intention. Many espouse "career concern," but as the research indicates, few are master of practicing it.

What Does A Career Equity Culture Look Like?

How do leaders begin to create an organization that provides professionals with unique learning, relationships, and engagement? How can we implement an approach that makes a lasting impact on our people and firm? How can we know that the career management investments we are making work? If you are asking these questions you are on the right track. The following section provides four (4) key conditions, when practiced consistently, that build a unique culture of mutual value.

Examples of organizations that are practicing these elements in an exceptional way are provided to support implementation in your firm. These organizations are held up not because they are perfect. Rather, they seek to be the best they can at helping professionals learn, grow, and expand their career assets. A diverse sample of firm sizes, industries, and geography were selected to illustrate that a career equity culture can be cultivated wherever there are thoughtful leaders who strive to make it possible.

CULTIVATING A CAREER EQUITY CULTURE

Condition 1: Link professional growth and retention to the firm's strategic plan and communicate it intentionally.

The Design Group, an entity of Barry-Wehmiller Inc., is a perfect example of a leadership team that is very purposeful about building a culture of career significance and puts promises into practice. The Design Group provides technical resources, engineering services, and industry-experienced insight for Fortune 500 companies internationally.

Managing Partner Joe Wilhelm and his leadership team are keenly aware of the relationship between professional growth, retention, and business results. Helping professionals build career equity is a daily practice. The firm has dedicated leadership resources to professional career growth and retention that are integral to the firm's strategic plan and superior to other conventional performance management systems used in the past.

During The Design Group's first two years of Career Equity implementation they achieved double-digit growth and retention of the best talent. Because of their success, parent company Barry-Wehmiller ($1B in revenue and more than 5,000 employees) is moving toward implementation of the Career Equity model.

To see how and what The Design Group leaders communicate to associates, consider the following excerpt from the managing partners' message to the firm:

The Design Group Career Development Program focuses on an annual Career Development Discussion (CDD) for every professional. **The purpose of the Career Development Discussion (CDD) is to align our professional's aspirations and the Firm's goals which will lead to a more fulfilling career experience.**

A Career Development Leadership Council which consists of eight leaders from across the firm who met to define and schedule the implementation of our new CDD process...which is centered on the concept of "Career Equity."

Career Equity is a concept designed to help professionals grow their careers. Career Equity is defined as *"the professional's stake, or equity, which is being built as their career develops."* The *Career Development Discussion* focuses on linking your daily activities, your investment of time and effort, and the firm's investment in you to the development of your personal Career Equity. We believe that as you increase your Career Equity, you will be able to increase the value of your contributions to the firm, and help build your stake in the future!

As an example a Design Group software engineer learns how to program a new software package (an investment)...which drives demand with our clients.

CULTIVATING A CAREER EQUITY CULTURE

> *This makes him more valuable both inside and outside the Firm...and gives him more control over future assignments. As a second example, a project manager is trained on "industry recognized" communication procedures (an investment)...these disciplines lead to more predictable results which makes him more valuable both inside and outside the Firm. This value allows him to lead larger and larger projects or with more complex clients.*
>
> *We believe there are five (5) main attributes that indicate how engaged a professional is in "actively developing" his or her own personal Career Equity:*
> - *Is the professional engaged in "meaningful and challenging" work?*
> - *Is the professional developing "meaningful relationships" internally or externally?*
> - *Is the professional "learning and growing" with each assignment?*
> - *Is the professional involved from a "community or culture" standpoint?*
> - *Is the professional recognized and rewarded fairly based on their contributions?*

Like other elements of organizational effectiveness, cultivating a Career Equity culture begins with leadership. The Design Group and other successful firms achieve great people-related business results because their leaders have a strong desire to offer professionals a unique career experience. These leaders communicate their intentions clearly, concisely, and most importantly, hold themselves accountable for making it real. How does your firm define and implement strategic goals for professional growth and development?

Commitment to career growth and investment is always being tested by professionals. As mentioned previously, many firm leaders say they are dedicated to professional growth but few in practice follow through on these words with consistent action. This is especially true during uncertain economic times. The press is replete with companies that abandon strategic people investments when revenue and profits shrink. While reducing time and resources in training, coaching, and other overhead costs seem logical, it is evidence of short-term thinking and sends a strong message about the firm's intentions that are difficult to counteract when economic times improve. Leaders who are truly committed to mutual career and organizational growth do so in anytime.

Protiviti is a leading global-risk consulting and internal audit firm of 2,500 employees across the world. The leaders of Protiviti are very clear that their vision to be the premier global-risk consulting and internal audit services firm demands cultivating career growth and retention of top-tier professionals relentlessly. Like other Career Equity–building firms, Protiviti's leaders have a clear definition of what career equity means, and they communicate this to employees:

> "Career Equity is all about building value in you professionally and helping you achieve things in your work that matter to you. We want everyone at Protiviti to be able to say:
> 1. I am given opportunities to learn, grow, and show what I can do.
> 2. I do work that is interesting and valued by my clients.
> 3. I team with people that I know and respect.
> 4. I am recognized for my efforts and rewarded for my performance.
> 5. My life is enriched through my association with Protiviti."
>
> *"Here at Protiviti we believe our careers are about more than just working, providing deliverables, and being compensated. Our work is about opportunities to lead, learn, grow, and make a difference for our clients. That is what energizes and inspires us."*
>
> —Scott Redfearn,
> vice president, Human Resources, Protiviti

Nancy Pechloff, St. Louis office managing director and leader of Protiviti's Best People and Culture Cornerstone Strategy for the Central Region, summed it up this way, "We are committed to fostering the career development of our people. In fact, Protiviti's internal mantra is *Grow, Strengthen, Succeed.*

BUILDING CAREER EQUITY

We do this by endeavoring to provide our people with challenging and interesting client projects and by staying connected to each person, so we can understand his or her interests."

Protiviti's People Cornerstone processes include purposeful biannual reviews in which the reviewee is asked to actively participate. This underscores the firm's belief that career growth and satisfaction are a co-owned responsibility between the professional and leadership. During these reviews, Protiviti leaders engage in an open dialogue with professionals about career aspirations, 360-degree feedback, progress on skills development and certifications, and their interests. They utilize the five elements of career equity to help identify where professionals are gaining value and where they may need to increase investments of time and attention. If you ask Nancy Pechloff why professionals value being part of the Protiviti team, she will tell you, "The key factors that bond our people to Protiviti include our unique culture and close personal relationships among Protiviti colleagues as well as with our clients."

How is your firm cultivating mechanisms for open, honest career dialogue? How often do they occur? Is your firm making strategic investments like The Design Group's Career Development Leadership Council or Protiviti's Best People and Culture Cornerstone strategy?

CULTIVATING A CAREER EQUITY CULTURE

Condition 2: Implement a systematic assessment of career satisfaction and develop action plans for improvement.

The shareholders and Executive Committee of Capes, Sokol, Goodman, & Sarachan, P.C., take building a Career Equity culture seriously. In addition to linking professional growth and retention to their strategic objectives, they do a great job of systematically surveying professionals to identify where the firm is honoring commitments and areas for continuous improvement. The following is a portion of their Semiannual Career Equity survey.

Semiannual Career Equity Firm Survey

Please rate your satisfaction by marking the point on the line that most corresponds with your response.

1. Appreciation and recognition of efforts/successes (my opinion is valued)

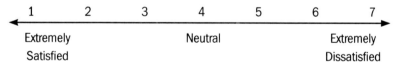

2. Professional growth through Bar involvement (firm support and sponsorship)

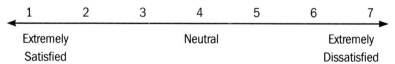

3. The role I play in cases

```
   1        2        3        4        5        6        7
◄──────────────────────────────────────────────────────────►
Extremely                  Neutral                  Extremely
Satisfied                                           Dissatisfied
```

4. The diversity of my work, cases, and experience

```
   1        2        3        4        5        6        7
◄──────────────────────────────────────────────────────────►
Extremely                  Neutral                  Extremely
Satisfied                                           Dissatisfied
```

5. Learning and growth through client seminars and other functions

```
   1        2        3        4        5        6        7
◄──────────────────────────────────────────────────────────►
Extremely                  Neutral                  Extremely
Satisfied                                           Dissatisfied
```

6. Collaboration between colleagues, partners, and staff

```
   1        2        3        4        5        6        7
◄──────────────────────────────────────────────────────────►
Extremely                  Neutral                  Extremely
Satisfied                                           Dissatisfied
```

7. Community involvement (firm support of my involvement or others)

```
   1        2        3        4        5        6        7
◄──────────────────────────────────────────────────────────►
Extremely                  Neutral                  Extremely
Satisfied                                           Dissatisfied
```

CULTIVATING A CAREER EQUITY CULTURE

8. Appreciation and recognition of efforts/successes
(my opinion is valued)

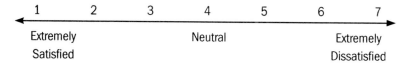

After collecting responses through an anonymous electronic survey, the results are reviewed in detail by the Executive Committee and all shareholders. The Executive Committee hosts a career development forum to share results with all associates and paralegals and identify priorities for action in the next six months.

What process does your organization use to systematically measure the career growth and satisfaction of professionals? What happens to feedback gathered? How do you know if you are making progress?

Another example of a firm that does an exceptional job of assessing the current state of Career Equity is ARCTURIS. ARCTURIS is one of the nation's top corporate architecture, planning, and interiors firms. For more than four years, firm leaders have been dedicated to cultivating a Career Equity culture and the results show it. Not only do firm leaders assess Career Equity satisfaction of every member of the firm, they engage the "Peoples Evolution" group to analyze results, recommend, and prioritize solutions that are most relevant to professionals at all levels of the firm. ARCTURIS leaders are high on accountability. Their Career Equity results are quantifiable, an integral part of the firm's strategic plan and influence a component of principal compensation.

Condition 3: Ensure that every professional has a Trusted Career Advisor or mechanism for feedback.
None of the Career Equity elements are more essential to creating a career-oriented culture for professionals than the presence of caring and challenging mentors or what I call "Trusted Career Advisors." Research on professional growth, development, retention, and advancement never fails to spotlight the importance of these career confidants.

As mentioned earlier, left to their own devices most professionals seek out career guidance and input from friends and peers. While emotional support from peers is comforting, career coaching from peers lacks several important components. First, peers, especially early in their career, lack experience or perspective to provide a long-term solution. In other words, they do not have the benefit of repetitive practice or consistent implementation.

Secondly, peer relationships are often focused more on support than on challenge. To advance a significant goal in any area of life, but especially one's career, means doing things that are uncomfortable. Trusted advisors, with experience and authority, can help push professionals out of their comfort zone to realize their next level of growth.

Finally, and most importantly, peers lack the authority to influence change needed. For example, if an employee is dissatisfied with the repetitive nature of their assignments, peers do not have the organizational authority to change their assignments. A manager or mentor does. Without purposeful and planned support from caring leaders, your best professionals run the risk of getting bad career advice 60 percent of the time.

Northwestern Mutual Financial Network is the only company to lead its industry as one of America's Most Admired Companies® for twenty-five consecutive years. The organization's business model is totally dependent on recruiting and retaining the best talent in the financial-security industry. Without financial representatives to serve policyholders Northwestern Mutual loses its competitive advantage.

Therefore, firm leaders are purposeful about the support and challenge each financial representative receives to fulfill his or her career aspirations. The Qualy Group is the #1 Northwestern Mutual agency in the United States which deploys multiple mentoring strategies to foster professional growth and retention (e.g., mentors, monthly client builder meetings, regular coaching from managing directors, etc.). One of the best examples of a systematic mentoring process is their Quarterly Board of Review. Chief Development Officer, Matt Plocher, ensures that each financial representative has the opportunity for a review by a Board that comprises the managing director, mentor(s), and the firm's development director. This group meets four times a year to review the professional's progress toward his or her business and career aspirations for the current fiscal year and his or her longer- term vision.

Each professional is required to present a report of his or her plan, goals, and results. Feedback from the Board is documented and forms the basis for monthly coaching and development. This highly customized and consistent forum for feedback is a unique and valued strategy for adding Career Equity to each professional's career portfolio.

Condition 4: Instill consistent follow-up and follow-through on career aspirations

Benjamin Franklin is known for saying "well done is better than well said." In cultivating an organizational culture, this could not be more true and relevant. Research by Jim Collins, internationally known author of *Good to Great,* reveals the best organizations achieve great results because their leaders execute strategy consistently. Leaders who desire short-term success can put this book down. You will not achieve the multiple benefits a Career Equity culture delivers. Only those who have the capacity to delay gratification and the confidence to persist in the face of doubt win at this game.

An example of how the leaders at RubinBrown, one of the nation's best and fastest growing accounting firms, consistently follow through on cultivating a Career Equity culture follows. Take note of the ways you and your firm leaders could instill this practice of regular talent reviews.

CULTIVATING A CAREER EQUITY CULTURE

Every quarter, like clockwork, Lynn Davis, director of Human Resources, and managing partner John Herber convene their key service line leaders for a review of the best talent in the firm. Utilizing formal performance review data, input from Career Development Counselors (CDCs), and mentors, the firm leaders assess the career aspirations and advancement potential of their best professionals. Specific actionable observations and plans are documented and Lynn is accountable for ensuring these strategies are fulfilled. What is the result? The firm has one of the best retention rates for accounting professionals and a deep pipeline of future leaders to fuel growth of new offices.

The purpose of this chapter is to equip you as a firm leader with the knowledge, tools and examples to begin cultivating a Career Equity culture. While the elements of Career Equity are consistent, the way each organization embraces and implements these practices vary widely. Creating a Career Equity culture is not a cookie-cutter effort. It enhances the unique culture firm leaders seek to differentiate themselves in an increasingly competitive marketplace for talent.

One of the best ways to get culture building underway is to ask firm leaders and professionals to complete the Career Equity Culture Assessment. Host a series of discussions about where your firm is today and which elements would make a significant difference to the career growth and satisfaction of professionals. Full culture change can take between three and five years. Set realistic expectations, organize a plan, and begin.

BUILDING CAREER EQUITY

Extra Credit for Firm Leaders:

1) Read Jay W. Lorsh and Thomas J. Tierney, *Aligning the Stars* (Boston: Harvard Business School Publishing, 2002).
2) Consult David Maister's, *Managing the Professional Services Firm* (New York: Free Press Paperbacks: A Division of Simon and Schuster Inc., 1993).
3) Read Jim Collins, *Good to Great* (New York: HarperCollins Publishers Inc., 2001).

Conclusions

"Success is a journey, not a destination. The doing is often more important than the outcome."
—*Arthur Ashe*

Building Career Equity, like life, is not a linear journey. Whether you are exploring these practices for yourself, your protégé(s), or have aspirations of building a Career Equity culture for your firm, the process begins with self-awareness and then immediately demands collaboration. Greater awareness lies in taking the time to answer fundamental questions about your career. For example, where have you accumulated the most career assets? What is energizing or easy for you? What needs a higher level of intention? How can you more fully realize your potential and make a difference in the lives of others?

If you take nothing else away from this book, I hope you see career growth and satisfaction as an interdependent process. No one achieves success in isolation. Career Equity master builders have a clear vision of where they want to go and work purposefully with clients, colleagues, leaders, and community organizations to make their vision a reality. Their stories, in retrospect, may sound logical and straightforward. If you do A then B will follow. In truth, everyone mentioned in this book, individually or organizationally, achieved success because they persisted in the face of delay, disappointment, and often rejection. At the same time, they sought feedback from people who cared about their growth and challenged them to do things that were neither comfortable nor familiar. They are building rich and rewarding careers because they never gave up and sought help in the pursuit of their aspirations.

Career Equity builders are experts at making and keeping commitments. They know that career significance is achieved over the long-term. They defy the current culture of instant gratification. They have their eye on a horizon of four to five years not four to five months. Time and time again, the effective people I know say that their most valuable career experiences are the most difficult ones. When confronted with a difficult situation, manager, or peer, they often thought of leaving or quitting. The difference is they didn't.

Thus, one piece of evidence you will see in the histories of Career Equity builders is tenure. What does your résumé communicate about your career? Does it reveal serial changes? At the turn of the century, frequent job changes were perceived to be a badge of honor. But like the dot.com bubble, that career strategy burst.

CONCLUSIONS

When you look at those who build significant careers, businesses, and lives, you will see a pattern of what one highly successful managing partner calls "long obedience in the same direction." Of course there are exceptions to every rule and factors beyond our control, but in the end, those who realize great satisfaction and impact stay for the time required to make a difference. Tenure is not a reflection of complacency or fear about leaving. Instead, it is a thoughtful decision aligned to long-term aspirations. As career opportunities arise, Career Equity builders consider how it will fit into their overall portfolio of experience, relationships, and rewards. Like the "buy and hold" philosophy of financial investing, building Career Equity demands a plan and commitment to stay the course in turbulent times.

The five factors of Building Career Equity provide the road map for achieving a long-term return on your investment of time, talent, and energy. In summary, Doing Engaging Work provides the framework for defining our aspirations and vision. The tools and practices in Chapter 2 help identify the skills and experiences that motivate us and provide a filter for evaluating potential career opportunities.

In Chapter 3, we discover how and why meaningful relationships influence our success and the strategies to cultivate more of the interactions we want. Few professionals stay committed to their career or organization without planned and purposeful learning. Therefore, Chapter 4 outlines five strategies for proactively managing a learning and development plan that keeps curiosity high and career assets current. Is giving back to the broader context of human affairs or community vital to you? Chapter 5, Contributing to Community offers tools, examples, and inspiration for how to get involved and concurrently build career capacity. Purposeful career strategy, relationships, learning, and giving have their rewards. Chapter 6 provides specific recommendations on how to increase the return on career investments by knowing the facts about salary, benefits, and potential for recognition.

While the five assets of Building Career Equity provide a powerful mental model and practical tools, it is the intentional implementation or "doing" as Arthur Ashe notes that makes the difference. If you struggle with following through on your career ambitions, re-read Chapter 7, Putting Action and Accountability Behind Aspirations. Pick one of the habits that speak to you and commit to utilize it for the next thirty days.

Chapter 8 was written specifically to and for firm leaders. It offers a toolkit for collaborating with professionals the organization most wants to attract and retain. Companies recognized as "best places to work" generously share how they implement the Building Career Equity formula. They have evidence of the firm's positive business results when they focus on helping professionals realize their career aspirations.

CONCLUSIONS

*"Boldness has genius, power, and magic in it. Only engage, and then the mind grows heated. **Begin it,** and the work will be completed."*

—*Johann Wolfgang von Goethe*

What is the first step you can take to act on this knowledge and learning? Who can help you convert dreams into tangible career experiences? What would it be like if everyone in your organization had a shared way of defining, discussing, and advancing their career goals?

I would value hearing from you about how Building Career Equity informed your career goals, aspirations, and, most importantly, action. E-mail jan@buildingcareerequity.com to promote the mutual and meaningful career growth of others.

Bibliography

Allen, David. *Getting Things Done.* New York: Penguin Group, 2001.

Babcock, Linda, and Sarah Laschever. *Women Don't Ask: Negotiation and the Gender Divide.* Princeton University Press, 2003.

Baker, Wayne E. *Achieving Success through Social Capital.* Jossey-Bass: August 2000.

Birlingham, Bo. *The Believer.* New York: Inc. magazine, August 2008.

Boldt, Lawrence G. *How to Find the Work You Love.* New York: Penguin Group, 1996.

Buckingham, Marcus and Donald O. Clifton. *Now Discover Your Strengths.* New York: The Free Press, 2001.

Butler, Timothy and James Waldroop. *Discovering Your Career in Business.* New York: Perseus Books, 1996.

Covert, Jack and Todd Satterson. *The 100 Best Business Books of All Time: What They Say, Why They Matter, And How They Can Help You.* New York: Penguin Group, 2009.

Covey, Stephen R. *The Seven Habits of Highly Effective People.* New York: Free Press of Simon & Shuster, 2004.

Covey, Stephen R. and Bob Whitman, Breck England. *Predictable Results in Unpredictable Times.* Salt Lake City, Utah: Franklin Covey, September 2009.

Csíkszentmihályi, Mihály. Flow: *The Psychology of Optimal Experience.* Harper Perennial Modern Classics: July 2008.

Drucker, Peter. *The Practice of Management.* New York: Harper Collins Publishers, Inc. October 1954.

Fischer, Donna. *People Power: 12 Power Principles to Enrich your Business, Career, & Personal Networks.* Marietta, Georgia: Bard Press, 1995.

Forni, P.M. *Choosing Civility: The Twenty-five Rules of Considerate Conduct.* New York: St. Martin's Press, February 2002.

Gladwell, Malcolm. *The Tipping Point: How Little Things Can Make A Big Difference.* Little, Brown and Company, March 2000.

Granovetter, Mark. *Getting a Job: A Study of Contacts and Careers.* University Of Chicago Press: March 1995.

Gray, Albert E. N. *The New Common Denominator of Success.* Books2Wealth Edition, Albany, OR: Albany Publishing Company, 2010.

Gualdoini, Claire. *The Greater Good: How Philanthropy Drives the American Economy and Can Save Capitalism.* New York: Times Books, 2003.

Hill, Napolean. *Think and Grow Rich.* The Random House Publishing Group: 1937.

BIBLIOGRAPHY

Kristie, James. "Boards at Their Best." Board Room Briefing, Winter, 2006.

Maister, David H. and Charles H. Green, and Robert M. Galford. *The Trusted Advisor.* New York: Touchstone, 2001.

Maxwell, John C. *Leadership Promises for Every Day.* Nashville, TN: Thomas J. Nelson Inc., 2003.

Rosenberg, Arthur D. *101 Ways to Stand Out at Work: How to Get the Recognition and Rewards You Deserve.* Adams Media and F+W Media Company, 2009.

CPSIA information can be obtained
at www.ICGtesting.com
Printed in the USA
FFOW05n2311100715